Bell's Comet

Bell's Comet

How a Paddle Steamer
Changed the Course of History

P.J.G. RANSOM

AMBERLEY

Front cover: A harbinger of change in a settled world: the newly commissioned *Comet* steams up the Firth of Clyde near Bowling in 1812, overtaking sailing ships as she does so.

Back cover: Henry Bell surmounted innumerable difficulties throughout his life; his honest, friendly face must surely have been the secret of his success.

First published 2012

Amberley Publishing
The Hill, Stroud
Gloucestershire, GL5 4EP

www.amberley-books.com

Copyright © P. J. G. Ransom 2012

The right of P. J. G. Ransom to be identified as the Author
of this work has been asserted in accordance with the
Copyrights, Designs and Patents Act 1988.

British Library Cataloguing in Publication Data.
A catalogue record for this book is available from the British Library.

ISBN 978 1 4456 0349 0

Typesetting and Origination by Amberley Publishing.
Printed in Great Britain.

Contents

Some other books by
P. J. G. Ransom

The Archaeology of Canals
The Archaeology of the Transport Revolution 1750-1850
Scottish Steam Today
Scotland's Inland Waterways
Loch Lomond and the Trossachs in History and Legend
Iron Road: The Railway in Scotland
Steamers of Loch Lomond
Old Arrochar and Loch Long.

Acknowledgements

I am most grateful for assistance rendered, and information provided, by the following:

Chris Alcorn, West Lothian Council; Valerie Boa, Inverclyde Council; Paul Bristow, Inverclyde Community Development Trust; Sybil Cavanagh, West Lothian Council; Michael Davis, Helensburgh Library; Clare Delgal and Debbie Francis, Institution of Civil Engineers; Derek Grindell; Jane Harrison, The Royal Institution of Great Britain; Rupa Kundu, British Science Association; John Liffen, Science Museum; Shaun Lundy, Inverclyde Council; Emily Malcolm, Riverside Museum, Glasgow; Campbell McCutcheon, Amberley Publishing; Jenny McGhie, East Renfrewshire Council; Eleanor McKay, Argyll & Bute Libraries; Stewart Noble, Comet Bicentenary Committee; Fiona Sharkey, Helensburgh Library; and the staffs of the Mitchell Library, Glasgow, the National Archives (Kew), the National Archives of Scotland and the National Library of Scotland.

My wife Elisabeth, my sons Robert and Hugh, and my agent Duncan McAra have been most supportive, as ever. Many thanks to all.

ONE

The First Powered Transport

Henry Bell is our least-known national hero. Remark to somebody: 'Bell – pioneer of communications', and the answer will be, as likely as not, an interrogative: 'Telephones?' What Henry Bell did, in 1812 on the Clyde with his paddle steamer *Comet,* was to establish a viable steamer service – the first in Britain. Indeed it was the first anywhere outside North America, where Robert Fulton had got in before him, establishing a successful steamer service in 1807 but using, readers of jingoistic inclination will be pleased to note, good British machinery supplied by Boulton, Watt & Co. It was Bell's pioneering venture, though, that was the starting point for rapid expansion in use of steamers around Britain, Europe and throughout the Old World.

The steamer, or steamboat as the early examples were generally called, was the first successful application of mechanical power to passenger transport.[1] Travellers by water were at last freed from dependence on the fickle effects of winds, currents, tides and oarsmen's muscles. Since most early steamboat services ran parallel to the coast, or on rivers, many travellers by land were similarly freed from the efforts of animals or Shanks' pony. It was a development comparable to the first use of the wheel. The engine of the *Comet* survived to reach, eventually, the Science Museum, South Kensington: there its significance is recognised by display not, as might have been the case, in an obscure section devoted to the details of marine engineering, but in a gallery entitled 'Making the Modern World'.

This development was also of huge economic importance. The coming of mechanical transport, wrote Henry Hamilton in *The Industrial Revolution in Scotland,* prepared the way for a vast expansion of commerce and, therefore, of industry – shipbuilding and engineering, particularly.[2] At a regional level, the arrival of the steamboat, according to John F. Riddell in his history of the Clyde Navigation, was an event of quite incalculable benefit, and almost overnight transformed Glasgow's status as a port.[3] Taking all of this into account, it is worth considering why Bell is not more famous than he is, why indeed he is not a household name. The clue, unfortunately, lies in the highly complex character of the man himself. Although his real achievement was solid enough, he was inclined to claim far more – particularly late in life, when there seemed some chance of a government grant to relieve straightened circumstances – and all his claims have to be considered in this light. There is more of this in subsequent chapters, but this difficulty, of sorting fact from fiction, probably explains why no biography of Bell was published during the century and a half between 1844 and 1995. This in turn must have contributed to lack of public awareness of the man and what he achieved.

However Bell, if largely forgotten nationally, is certainly celebrated as a local hero. There is a prominent memorial, and relics of his activities, to be seen in his home town of Helensburgh; on the opposite shore of the Clyde, a full-size replica of *Comet* is displayed in Port Glasgow close to the location where the original was built. In former times he was remembered even better. The *Comet* centenary in 1912 came at the period when Glasgow and the Clyde were near the peak of prosperity. The corporation came together with other local authorities, public bodies and so on to organise a programme of celebrations of which the climax was a review of the fleet – consisting of everything from warships to dredgers – by dignitaries assembled on the deck of the Clyde's most famous paddle steamer, *Columba*, while an associated exhibition at Kelvingrove Museum required an 83-page catalogue to describe fully all the 451 items on display. At this period Karl Baedeker was reminding his readers that two-thirds of all British steamers were built, or at least provided with their engines, on the Clyde. Giving credit to their originator he added, with absolute accuracy, that the first steamer on this side of the Atlantic was placed on the Clyde by Henry Bell in 1812 and plied between Glasgow and Greenock.[4]

This year of 1812 is remarkable in that it saw not only the emergence of the steamboat, but also that of the steam railway locomotive into commercial service. The locomotives concerned were the work of Matthew Murray, built for the Middleton Railway at Leeds. But they did not haul passengers: rather they lumbered along with waggons of coal. It would be almost two decades before the locomotive was developed far enough to be practicable for haulage of passengers, and the Middleton locomotives did not have the same immediate widespread consequences as did the *Comet*. However their appearance on the scene became known very quickly to John Thomson, one of Bell's associates, and almost certainly to Bell himself.[5]

Construction of *Comet* and subsequent steamboats at this date was much aided by the presence in Glasgow of engineers already practised in building steam engines to power mills and factories, and by the presence on the Clyde of experienced builders of ships – wooden ships, for use of iron as a material for building ships was then in its infancy. On the other hand, it was hindered by limited, though developing, understanding of the properties of heat. And operation of steam engines on land was still a novelty, compared with the centuries, indeed millennia, of accumulated experience in operating sailing vessels on the water. Remarkably, few if any professional sailors are to be found among the ranks of those who invented or attempted to invent steamboats, despite the evident need. Bell himself was a builder.

Design and construction of sailing vessels had developed over the centuries. In Britain, since the latter part of the eighteenth century harbours had been improved, and canals built. Along the canals boats were tracked by horses, to bring the benefits of water transport inland, complementing existing rivers and lakes. Elsewhere on land, people had formerly travelled on foot or horseback, and goods were carried on pack horses, along routes which would seem to us no more than tracks: by the end of the eighteenth century roads wide enough and smooth enough for coaches and waggons had been built, and coach services introduced. But, at the time when Bell started to think about a steamboat, the process still had far to go: Telford's road improvements were under way, McAdam's had scarcely started, the Caledonian Canal, the deepest and widest in Britain at this period, was still far from complete.

Stationary steam engines, at the date when Bell decided to have his steamboat built, had already been in use for almost exactly a century: it had been in 1712 that the first of Thomas Newcomen's pumping engines had been installed, to drain a coal mine in the West Midlands. Strictly speaking this and its immediate successors were atmospheric engines: pressure of the atmosphere drove a piston downwards into a cylinder when a partial vacuum was formed below the piston by sudden condensation of steam beneath it. The piston was connected to one end of a huge wooden beam, centrally pivoted: to the other end was attached the pump rod. Piston goes down, pump rod comes up; more steam admitted into the bottom of the cylinder, weight of pump rod and attachments takes it down while piston rises. A jet of water into the cylinder condenses the steam, and the cycle starts over again. And so on, indefinitely. The whole apparatus was as big as a house. Literally, for the cylinder and associated parts were built into a house with the beam pivoted on one of the walls.

Alternately admitting steam to the cylinder and then condensing it meant heating the cylinder up and then cooling it, over and over again. That used a lot of steam, which meant using a lot of fuel. It took James Watt (1736–1819), native of Greenock and instrument maker to Glasgow University, to think out the solution to this problem: when the piston was at the top of its stroke, let the steam into another vessel and condense it there, while keeping the cylinder hot. He patented the 'separate condenser' early in 1769. But for an instrument maker to transform this concept from elegant idea to the massive reality of the Newcomen engine was far from straightforward. It needed funding, and accurate workmanship. An initial partnership with Dr John Roebuck, one of the founders of the Carron Ironworks near Falkirk, collapsed when Roebuck became insolvent.[6]

Watt then turned to Matthew Boulton, respected Birmingham manufacturer of high-quality metal goods – buttons, buckles, toys, sword hilts and the like. Fortuitously, also in this period the ironmaster John Wilkinson had just developed machinery for boring cannon barrels accurately. Watt was able to use a cylinder supplied by Wilkinson, bored on this equipment, to set up the first satisfactory engine made to his patent. He did so at Boulton's Soho Manufactory where its task was to pump back, during times of shortage, water used by the waterwheel which powered the works. Watt entered into a formal partnership with Boulton in 1775, having first had his patent extended to run until 1800, and the Soho engine proved to be the first of many. Boulton & Watt did the design work and manufactured small parts; large parts were provided by outside suppliers, and the entire engines were erected on site by skilled erectors trained by the partnership. Users paid royalties based on estimated fuel savings.

At this period Watt's fertile brain was considering many other potential improvements to the atmospheric engine. One of them was to close in the top of the cylinder, with the piston rod passing through the cover. The engine could then be made double-acting, with steam admitted above the piston while it was being condensed below, and so on. That in turn raised the possibility of using steam at pressure higher than atmospheric – although not very much higher, for manufacturing techniques would not yet allow it. Watt patented the double-acting engine in 1782, and the first was built the following year.

The double-acting principle, in which both up and down strokes were powered, greatly facilitated development of the rotative engine. What had been the pump rod was instead attached to a crank mounted on a shaft to which it gave rotary motion. The principle of the crank was ancient, but another inventor had got in first and patented its application to the steam engine – Watt invented, and patented, his own methods. The possibilities of the rotative engine for powering machinery were almost limitless. Boulton & Watt installed their first rotative engines in 1782–3; customers paid an annual levy based on horsepower. But Watt's preference seems to have been to exploit existing applications to the full. He was initially hesitant about exploiting rotative engines, and it seems to have been at the insistence of Boulton, who understood how large the market would be, that he did so.

The first large-scale application of steam engines to drive machinery was at the Albion Mills, London, in the late 1780s. These mills were intended to be huge by the standards of the time – there were to be thirty pairs of stones compared with four in the next largest flour mill in London, and Boulton & Watt had the contract for steam engines and milling machinery. To supervise erection of this, they employed John Rennie (1761–1821).[7] Rennie, son of an East Lothian tenant farmer, had gained practical experience of machinery from working with Andrew Meikle, gifted local millwright and inventor of the threshing machine, and he had studied at Edinburgh University under John Robison, the distinguished professor of natural philosophy.[8] He was already in business as an engineer. Robison and Watt were old friends, and it appears to have been this link which cemented the relationship between Watt and Rennie. Rennie did not become a full-time employee in the long term – there seems to have been an informal arrangement in which Boulton & Watt recommended him to their customers to design and build the machinery which their steam engines were to drive, and Rennie equally recommended to his machinery customers that they should use Boulton & Watt engines to drive it. Rennie also seems to have acted as Boulton & Watt's eyes and ears as he travelled about Britain. Eventually his career broadened to include bridges, canals, docks, engineering consultancy and much else, including steamboats – he became one of the most famous civil engineers of the early nineteenth century. (The term 'civil engineers' in those days implied civil rather than military, and embraced those who would later become known as 'mechanical engineers'.) The Albion Mills meantime had become initially one of the sights of London, but management was bad and regrettably in 1791 an overheated bearing caused a fire which lasted three days and burned out the building. But the principle of using steam engines to drive machinery was established.

Steam engines needed boilers to supply them with steam, and these initially amounted to little more than tanks of water, closed in at the top and with a fire underneath. One popular early type was known from its shape

– a vertical cylinder with a dome above – as the 'haystack': it looked like the haystacks of the period. A slightly later type was the 'waggon': long and rectangular, with a horizontal half-cylinder on top, its shape was that of the covered waggons then familiar to every road user. Material was copper, or wrought iron; a brickwork surround kept burning gasses close to the boiler itself while en route from fire to chimney.

From the mid-1790s Watt's son James Watt junior (1769–1848) and Boulton's son Matthew Robinson Boulton took an increasing share of responsibility for running the business, and in 1795–6 a new works, Soho Foundry, was built specifically to manufacture steam engines. In 1800 James Watt retired and about the same time the firm became styled 'Boulton, Watt & Co.'[9] By then, of the 496 engines which Boulton & Watt had built, 308 were rotative.[10] In Scotland they were in use in cotton mills, corn mills, flax mills and other industries.[11]

Nevertheless, James Watt had opposed developing their evident potential for powering vehicles on land and vessels on water. He of all people was all too well aware of just how much hard graft was needed to turn an imaginative idea into practical reality. He seems with the passage of time to have become the expert who knew what could not be done. He was also assiduous in guarding his patent rights, and had good reason to be. Payment of regular royalties or fees soon came to be resented by users of Boulton & Watt engines: there was therefore a ready market for steam engines which evaded Watt's patents, or at least appeared to do so, and by the last decade of the century there were plenty of other engine builders who were willing to supply. Nevertheless the only engineer who was wholly successful in this was the noted Cornishman Richard Trevithick (1771–1833), who evaded Watt's master patent by simply eliminating the condenser, using 'strong steam' at pressures as high as 50 lb/sq. in., and exhausting used steam to the atmosphere.

With the development of the rotative engine, the steam engine had become free-standing, with the beam no longer pivoted upon a wall of the building but upon a massive timber framework. By the turn of the century cast iron was replacing wood for engine components, large and small. Leading the way in this was the Leeds firm of Fenton Murray & Wood. The engineering genius here was Matthew Murray (1765–1826), and by the mid-1790s he was building steam engines, and gaining a reputation for excellent quality. 'This man makes very free with your patents' reported John Rennie to Boulton & Watt in 1797, 'would it not be well to look sharply after him?'[12] They did not do so immediately but, when Murray applied for a patent for steam engine improvements in 1801, Boulton, Watt & Co. contested it with success. In the meantime, finding that the quality of Murray's cast iron components exceeded that of their own, James Watt junior and Matthew Robinson Boulton had been resorting to industrial espionage to discover his secrets.[13]

None of this prevented Murray from making important developments in the design of the steam engine. He invented the 'D' slide valve, for admission of steam to the cylinder and release from it, in the form which would become familiar world-wide.[14] He introduced a bedplate of cast iron, upon which were mounted cast iron supports for cylinder, beam and other components: the engine became an independent unit, no longer built into the structure of the engine house.[15] This meant that the engine could be very much more compact than previously. He patented a smooth-running two-cylinder engine with the cranks at right angles to one another.[16] He produced a compact engine with its main components supported upon a cistern containing the condenser,[17] and then developed the concept further in 1805 into an engine with the beam positioned below the cistern, driven by rods which passed either side of the cylinder and were connected above it to a crosshead on the piston rod. This he described as a 'portable steam engine', that is to say it could if desired be moved from place to place – it required 'no framing or mill-wright work in the fixing, but merely bolting down to the floor it stands upon.'[18]

Murray was paving the way for those who would design and build the first marine steam engines to be used commercially – starting with the *Comet*'s – as will be told in later chapters. First it is necessary to look at the many earlier attempts to make steamboats.

TWO

Steamboats Before Bell

Like flight, in the air or through space, the boat propelled by steam power was something of which people were aware as a possibility for many years, indeed decades, before it became reality. It was wholly appropriate that the American James Thomas Flexner gave his book on the subject the title *Steamboats Come True*. No single person invented the steamboat: it was the work, successively, of innumerable dreamers and schemers and practical men. And sometimes of people who were all three of these at once. The wisest among them drew heavily on the work of those who had gone before. Nearly all of them came from one of three countries: France, Great Britain, and the United States of America (in alphabetical order!). Space permits only the most significant individuals to be mentioned here.

The earliest pioneers

The first definite proposal for a steamboat was made as early as 1690 by Denis Papin, a French protestant refugee in London. He envisaged that a piston in a steam cylinder would be connected to paddle wheels to propel it.[1] Paddle wheels, driven by animal power, had been known since antiquity[2] – although that would not prevent many subsequent would-be inventors of the steamboat from using other means of propulsion. Papin was the first of many to tackle the subject. One of them was Jonathan Hulls, who in 1736 obtained a patent for a 'machine' to carry ships into or out of harbour against wind or tide or in a calm. It was to comprise a boat containing a Newcomen engine driving a paddle wheel, and towing the ship.[3] Hulls had identified an important role for the steamboat, but he was ahead of his time.

The first experimenter to achieve success (at his second attempt) in building a steamboat was the Marquis de Jouffroy D'Abbans. In 1778 his steamboat *Pyroscaphe* ascended the River Saône for a quarter of an hour. This however was not enough to attract support from the French government, and the revolution soon interrupted further work.[4]

In the 1780s the pace started to increase. In 1787 or thereabouts, Robert Fourness (or Furnace) and James Ashton built a steamboat, driven by paddle wheels, which they operated on the river between Hull and Beverley, Yorkshire. They are said to have followed this with a larger version, which was sent to London and bought by the Prince of Wales, but soon afterwards destroyed by fire. They did take out a patent for a steam engine in 1788.[5] But details of their work are hard to come by. The same cannot be said of the next persons to be considered, William Symington, together with Patrick Miller and James Taylor, with whom he was associated.

Symington, Miller and Taylor

William Symington (1764–1831) was a native of Leadhills, Lanarkshire. His elder brother George was engineer to the old-established lead mines at nearby Wanlockhead, and William had assisted him, initially as apprentice, when a Boulton & Watt engine was set up in 1779 to drain the mines. Coal was expensive in that district, which encouraged development of an engine more economical to run, and William Symington had designed an improved atmospheric engine which, he considered, evaded Watt's separate condenser patent and the need to pay premiums for use of this. Watt of course thought otherwise, but he was far away and many engines of Symington's type were eventually built.[6]

Patrick Miller (1731–1815) was a wealthy man, a director of the Bank of Scotland with fingers in many influential pies including, particularly relevant here, substantial interests in the Carron Company (established near Falkirk in 1759 as the first ironworks in Scotland to use coal rather than wood to smelt the iron) and in the Forth & Clyde Canal, by then open from the Forth at Grangemouth through Falkirk and almost to Glasgow.[7] He was also a man given to enthusiasms which often did not last long but were strong in the meantime. One of these was the development of ships to be driven by paddle wheels, turned by men working capstans, when the wind failed. He had been to sea as a young man. On trials James Taylor, who was tutor to

Miller's sons, took his turn on the capstan: exhausting work. He suggested using a steam engine, and he recommended Symington, who had been a school companion.[8]

The upshot was that Symington and Taylor built a small steam engine at Wanlockhead with the aid of a watchmaker – watch- and clock-makers were the precision engineers of the day. The engine was fitted into a small double-hulled steamboat, for trials on the loch at Dalswinton, Miller's Dumfriesshire estate. The engine was ingenious but complex: two upright cylinders working on the atmospheric principle, their pistons – which rose and fell alternately – being joined by a chain passing over a pulley above. Ratchet-and-pawl arrangements converted the alternating motion of this pulley into rotary motion for the paddle wheels. Symington's condensing system was fitted.[9]

The boat was tried out on the loch over several days in October 1788. Accounts have varied down the years as to just how well it worked. The artist Alexander Nasmyth, who was present, stated that Miller 'often had the pleasure of sailing with parties of his friends, by the power of this small steam engine'. James Cleland, deriving his information from another eye-witness, stated that the engine 'was so inefficient as occasionally to require the assistance of manual labour at a windlass'[10]. Such statements are not mutually exclusive: it has ever been a characteristic of the steam engine to perform well at one time but less so at another, as anyone who has suffered a clinkered-up firebox in a small steam launch is only too well aware. Symington himself later wrote that the boat 'gave such satisfaction that it was immediately determined to commence another experiment on a more extended scale.'[11]

The 'experiment on a more extended scale' took place during 1789. An enlarged version of the Dalswinton engine, with cylinders of 18-inch diameter and 3-foot stroke, was built at Carron Ironworks and fitted into one of Miller's vessels used previously for experiments with paddle wheels driven by capstans. With inevitable delays it was, probably, November before it was ready for trials. Symington and Taylor took her onto the Forth & Clyde Canal, and Miller and a party of Carron Company officials embarked. Spectators crowded the banks. After passing Lock 16 – the top lock of the flight by which the canal ascends through Falkirk – Symington went cautiously for a while, then gave the engine full play: it proved so powerful that the arms of the paddle wheels started to give way, and one float after another broke off. Stronger paddle wheels were made and fitted, and on 26 December, and again on 27 December, further trials were made with great success and a speed of nearly 7 mph achieved.[12]

But Miller was not there. When Taylor reported on these trials to him, the response was that he was to have the vessel dismantled.[13] On 7 December Miller had already written to Taylor expressing the view that Symington's engine was unsuitable for boats, for 'do as you will, a great deal of power of the engine must be lost in friction'[14]. But there was more to it than that. He had, it seems, been in touch with Boulton & Watt since the spring of 1788.[15] And James Watt had the details of Symington's 1789 engine, for John Rennie had seen it at Carron and reported back to him.[16] In the spring of 1790 Miller approached Boulton & Watt again, through the intermediary of his lawyer, Robert Cullen, later the noted judge Lord Cullen. Evidently he invited their co-operation in developing steam navigation. In his reply, on 24 April, James Watt wrote:

> ... From what we have heard of Mr Symington's engines, we are disposed to consider them as attempts to evade our exclusive privilege; but as we thought them so defective ... as not to be likely to do us immediate hurt, we thought it best to leave them to be judged by Dame Nature first, before we brought them to an earthly court.

In other words, if Miller persisted with Symington, Watt would sue. Watt also declined to enter into any sort of partnership in any new concern – Boulton & Watt had more than enough conventional business already – although they would supply rotative engines to Miller 'at our customary prices'. However he considered there would be 'considerable difficulty' in making them work satisfactorily on a ship rolling at sea.[17] All this seems to have been enough to divert Miller's future enthusiasms away from steam, and into agricultural improvements. Neither he nor Watt could know what was happening at just this time in America.

John Fitch and others

In the late eighteenth century, the potential for the steamboat was even greater in North America than in Britain and France. There, places up and down the East coast, between which movement was easy by sea-going sailing ship, were already settled, so pioneers were moving inland. Distances were great, roads scarce, rivers broad and long but lacking in towpaths. Here was the need. But to meet it America lacked the heavy industries already developing fast in Britain. The Newcomen atmospheric engine had reached North America only in 1753, when one was imported to drain a copper mine, and even then it took eighteen months to get it into position and into service.[18] What America did have was skilled artisans, gunsmiths and other workers in metal. One of them was John Fitch.

Fitch was a New Englander; he had been apprenticed to a clockmaker and became a skilled brassfounder and silversmith. Later he had moved to the western frontier where he attempted to trade with a raft going down the Ohio River. There he was captured by Indians, with whom he spent some time: a Stone-Age experience from which he was lucky to escape eventually with his life.[19]

Around 1785, back in the East, Fitch conceived the idea of propelling a boat by steam power, apparently at first believing this to be an original thought. Several years of painstaking work by trial and error followed, during the course of which he at one stage favoured propulsion by a series of paddles on each side of a boat, Indian-canoe style. He consulted those who had built Newcomen engines in America, enlisted the help of watchmaker Henry Voight and gathered the support of various financial backers. By 1787, when Miller was still experimenting with capstan-driven paddle wheels, Fitch achieved a boat which would move through the water – but no faster than 3 mph. Further development was needed. At last, in April 1790, by which date Symington's second steamboat was already laid up, Fitch achieved success with a steamboat driven by three vertical paddles which scooped water away from its stern. On trial on the Delaware River on a day of very fresh wind, no other boat, sailed or rowed, could keep up with her. 'We reigned Lord high admirals of the Delaware', recorded a delighted Fitch.[20]

It was the high point of his career. When the boat was put onto service to carry people between Philadelphia and Trenton, which it did for much of that summer, the passengers did not come. Or at least, not in sufficient numbers to make it a paying proposition. Probably the people of the time were just too conservative in their habits.[21]

To the cultured people of Philadelphia, already a great city,[22] Fitch may have seemed too much the archetypal backwoodsman. More plausible was his contemporary and competitor James Rumsey – an urbane innkeeper with contacts and backers far more distinguished than Fitch.[23] As early as 1784 he had made a model of a powered boat – a double-hulled vessel with, between the hulls, a water wheel, driven by the current and driving poles which engaged the river bed to propel the boat, punt-like, upstream.[24] Knowledge of this may have started Fitch thinking; it is unlikely that he took much else of his ideas from Rumsey.

By the late 1780s Rumsey was experimenting with water jet propulsion for boats: a steam pump was to draw water in near the bow, and expel it at the stern to drive the boat forward. The system was favoured by Benjamin Franklin, and Rumsey built a small boat on this principle with some success in 1787. His backers then sent him to England to develop the idea further. In 1788 Rumsey attempted and failed to reach agreement with Boulton & Watt. He then had a large hull built at Dover, and work started in 1790, in London, in equipping it with steam plant. But this was being done against increasing financial problems, and later that year Rumsey was in hiding from his creditors with work at a standstill. In 1792 matters had improved enough for work to restart, but sadly that December Rumsey died suddenly from apoplexy. The boat was completed by surviving partners, and tried out on the Thames a couple of months later, with some degree of success but not, it seems, enough for anyone to put it into regular service.[25]

Meanwhile, back in the USA, others were taking the steamboat idea forward. Notable among them were John Stevens, who had earlier supported Fitch, and his brother-in-law Robert Livingston – both of them wealthy landowners.[26] Livingston, in experiments in 1797, had the assistance of Marc Isambard Brunel, a French royalist *émigré* who had risen to become Chief Engineer of New York.[27] All will reappear in the story.

Also present in Philadelphia in the 1780s was a young Robert Fulton (1765–1815). He as yet showed no sign of the pivotal role he was to play in bringing the steamboat to fruition: he was working as an artist, a painter of miniatures. Late in 1786, probably, he set off for London to pursue this occupation, aided by an introduction to Benjamin West, the distinguished American artist who had preceded him and had risen to become president of the Royal Academy. Fulton himself exhibited there in 1791 and again two years later.[28] Then, in 1793, apparently while in the West Country on a painting commission, he decided to move from portraiture to engineering, and particularly canals[29]: this was the height of the English canal mania,[30] which may have drawn his attention to the subject in a general way.

Specifically though, his attention was drawn to it by 'perusing a paper descriptive of a canal projected by the Earl of Stanhope'.[31] This was the Bude Canal which Lord Stanhope, to whom we will return shortly, was then promoting. Fulton entered into correspondence with Stanhope in 1793,[32] and in the correspondence there appears for the first time a definite interest in steamboats – although while in London he had moved in the same circles as Rumsey,[33] so the subject may have come to his attention then. But canal engineering was his main preoccupation. In this one can see how his method of working developed. He was adept at assimilating the ideas of others, and quick to do so. On his return to London he met Thomas Telford, one of the foremost canal engineers of the age. Later, when Fulton published his ideas on canals in *A Treatise on the Improvement of Canal Navigation* (1796), which was a digest of many of the most advanced concepts on the subject, it contained so much of Telford's work, unacknowledged, as to leave a lasting legacy of ill-feeling.[34]

In 1794 Fulton travelled north, to Manchester and Worsley, cradle of the English canal system. He is said to have had an introduction to the Duke of Bridgewater, the great Canal Duke himself.[35] He may have discussed steamboats with him – there was an experimental steamboat, mentioned below, in the district. He did, that December, send a broad-based enquiry about steamboat engines to Boulton & Watt. They seem not to have deigned to reply.[36]

Later, after more canal work, Fulton set off in 1797 for France.[37] As an American he was entitled to do so, despite the war between Britain and France, although that did not make for easy travel.

The Earl of Stanhope

Charles, third Earl of Stanhope (1753–1816), is one of those maverick characters who enliven a tale such as this: an aristocrat, well-connected, yet of republican inclination and technical bent. He was responsible for substantial and lasting improvements in printing machinery; his attempts to do the same for steam navigation were in the end less successful.[38] But they started well. He was a fascinated visitor to Albion Mills, and consulted John Rennie on matters technical ever afterwards. He experimented with small steamboats, and in the course of these experiments invented the split pin. He inspected Rumsey's boat in London.

In 1792 he arranged with the Admiralty – the First Lord was his brother-in-law – to build a steamboat according to his plans and, if it proved satisfactory, bear the cost of doing so. The vessel was built in 1792–3 and the boiler installed in 1795. The vessel type he described as the 'ambi-navigator', since the hull was bi-directional, and the vessel could go into the wind as well as with it. The name of the actual boat was *Kent*.

The method of propulsion which Stanhope favoured was a pair of hardwood-and-iron paddles imitating the action of a duck's feet, placed under the boat's quarters. Unsurprisingly, as it now seems, this was in the end less than wholly satisfactory. No more than 3 mph could be achieved, although the vessel was found to sail well. The Admiralty did eventually pay the bills; the engine was removed and stored, and the hull broken up about 1798.[39]

The Bridgewater Canal

The experimental steamboat which Fulton probably heard of, and may have seen, near Manchester was the work of John Smith of St Helens. In 1793 he had fitted an atmospheric engine into a boat which made its first excursion down the St Helens Canal that June, laden with passengers bound for the races. Subsequently it crossed the Mersey to Runcorn and steamed up the Bridgewater Canal to Manchester before thousands of spectators.[40]

Among those spectators was a Mr Sherratt whose firm, Bateman & Sherratt, was doing a 'roaring trade' – according to Matthew Robinson Boulton – in engines which contravened Watt's condenser patent, until Boulton & Watt served an injunction on them in 1796.[41] Nevertheless it was to this firm that the Duke of Bridgewater turned when he decided to try out steam propulsion for himself on the Bridgewater Canal. The vessel to receive it was designed by a distinguished naval officer, Capt. John Schank (1740–1823), with whom the duke had had earlier dealings. Schank's long career had included many deeds of valour, but more relevant here was a justified reputation for mechanical ingenuity, particularly in design of vessels for use in shallow water. As early as 1774 he had invented the 'sliding keel', a type of centreboard, which was so effective that it had become a regular feature of shallow-draught naval vessels.

The steamboat, intended to tow coal boats from Worsley into Manchester, was built at Worsley with work starting in 1796. It had a single paddle wheel, mounted outboard, at the stern. Astern of that again was the rudder, and the tiller, so the helmsman cannot have been able to see much of what lay ahead. Unfortunately, when the boat was completed in 1799 its performance was less impressive than its provenance might have suggested. It successfully towed eight loaded boats into Manchester, but at only 1 mph. The blades of the paddle wheel caused much splashing and disturbance of the water, damaging the clay puddle which waterproofed the bed and banks of the canal. The boat did not go into regular service.[42] Nevertheless, Schank would be concerned in the next boat to be considered.

Charlotte Dundas

James Watt's patent on the separate condenser expired in the spring of 1800.[43] Within a matter of days, or perhaps even before its formal expiry, William Symington had been approached to build another steamboat. This time the approach came from Thomas, Lord Dundas, Governor of the

Company of Proprietors of the Forth and Clyde Navigation – the Forth & Clyde Canal, that is. The canal was now open from sea to sea, with a branch into Glasgow; at each end were flights of locks, but there was, and is, a long summit level and along this, and the branch into Glasgow, a steamboat would be valuable to haul the sloops and scows which used the canal. Dundas was aware of Symington's earlier work for Miller. The eventual boat, or boats, would be named, after his daughter, *Charlotte Dundas*.[44]

Boat, or boats: although this episode is well known, there has always been uncertainty about its details. For whatever reason, Symington in his own account refers only to a 'series of experiments' culminating in technical triumph.[45] He does not mention that the 'series of experiments' involved construction of first one steamboat and then another, nor that both were given the same name. Historians have ever since been confused about whether there was one boat or two and, if two, which events and incidents refer to which boat, in what sequence and at which date. What follows is believed by the author to have been the case, but interpretations have differed over the years.[46]

The skeleton of the story can, however, be established from J. and W. H. Rankine's 1862 biography of Symington, and more particularly from the copies of sworn affidavits which it contains.[47] These were made by Carron personnel, by shipbuilders, by Symington's own employees on board, and by a mariner; they were made in the mid-1820s when Symington, in reduced circumstances, was seeking financial aid from the government. From them it is clear that in 1801 Symington was employed by Dundas to erect a boat and construct a steam engine to propel it along the Forth & Clyde Canal, and that he afterwards constructed a larger steamboat. That was sworn by Joseph Stainton, who was a partner in, and manager of, Carron Ironworks at the time concerned,[48] and who added that he had seen both boats. From other affidavits it is evident that Alexander Hart in 1801 had built a boat 'of peculiar construction' for Symington, and assisted in installing a steam engine in it. Components for this were made at Carron Ironworks, according to pattern-makers William and James Blackie. James knew that the boat had moved 'a considerable number of miles' upon the canal. Robert Weir, who was the fireman, remembered it dragging two vessels along the Forth & Clyde Canal.

In 1802, according to an affidavit by John Allan, Symington instructed him to build a boat, also 'of peculiar construction', and he assisted in placing a steam engine in it, prior to the boat's removal to the canal. John Espline swore that in 1803 he had been master of the sloop *Euphemia* en route from

Grangemouth to Port Dundas, Glasgow, with a full cargo. She and the sloop *Active*, also deeply loaded, were taken in tow above Lock 20 by a steamboat superintended by Symington: this then towed them to Port Dundas, 19½ miles, in 6 hours. Alexander Sclanders, on oath like all the others, confirmed this, stating that he was helmsman on the *Charlotte Dundas* steamboat, that the month was March, and that 'it blew a strong breeze right ahead while on the passage; so much so, that no other vessels of any description could move to the windward in the Canal that day.' To those familiar with the climate of central Scotland in March, that last statement has the ring of conviction!

It is possible to enlarge on the story from other sources.[49] Construction of the steamboat had been approved on 5 June 1800 at a poorly-attended meeting of the governor and company, in London, expenses to be defrayed by the company. It was to be built according to a model by Captain Schank, which the governor showed to the meeting.[50] It would be interesting to know what form that model took. It is a reasonable guess that it was an advance on the rather ungainly Bridgewater Canal vessel, although perhaps not very much, bearing in mind that the Forth & Clyde Canal was both deeper and wider than the Bridgewater. Nor is much known about the layout of the engine. Carron invoiced the Forth & Clyde Navigation Co. on 30 June for the metal components of a steam engine – cylinder, piston and a host of lesser items – at a cost of £153 7s 1d, and added a further £22 4s 6d-worth on 7 August. These were, presumably, for the steamboat engine. There is little to indicate its layout. The list included '2 small gudgeons for the beam'; the beam itself, and the framework of the engine, were presumably of wood.[51]

The resultant boat was, however, effective enough not only to tow vessels along the canal, but also to go down onto the Forth to collect sloops detained by contrary wind and bring them into the canal. But the canal's committee of management – meeting in Scotland and often at odds with the governor – feared damage to the banks from its wash. Maybe the reputation of Schank's Bridgewater steamboat had preceded it. This was sufficient for its use to be discontinued.[52]

By then Symington was well advanced with work on the second boat, with Dundas evidently encouraging him,[53] (although he would eventually have to settle some of the accounts). Why they followed this course of action can scarcely now be explained. Maybe they thought that, if they provided a sufficiently convincing demonstration, the committee of management would be won over. Certainly the second *Charlotte Dundas* was a great technical advance. Although the boiler, a waggon-top type with flues built around it with bricks, was conventional enough, the engine which Symington provided, with parts made by Carron, had its cylinder horizontal, or nearly so, with direct drive by connecting rod to a crank on the paddle shaft (there may at times have been gears interposed between crankshaft and paddle shaft, presumably to establish the best relationship between engine speed and paddle wheel speed).[54] The horizontal cylinder, at that date, was revolutionary: only Trevithick, far away in Cornwall, was attempting the same.[55] Conventional wisdom of the period was that any cylinder position other than vertical would result in excessive wear of the bore and/or the piston.

The layout of the hull appears to be a development of Schank's ideas. The paddle wheel itself was positioned in a large recess in the stern – which looks like an attempt to minimise wash and bank erosion. This meant having, in effect, a double stern with a rudder each side of the paddle wheel: the helmsman stood in the bow, with a clear view ahead, working a sort of capstan which was connected to the rudders.

The second *Charlotte Dundas* made at least one earlier voyage through to Port Dundas before the triumphal one in March. Crowds turned out to see her. Technically, she was what was needed. But once again, like her predecessor, she did not go into regular service. The committee of management proved adamant. They had some justification. When powered boats were eventually put into regular service on canals of restricted dimensions, a vast amount of bank protection work was to be needed. But there was more to it. There appears to have been a power struggle building up between Dundas, who held the largest individual shareholding, and many of the other canal proprietors. Symington seems to have been an innocent victim of this. After festering for many years matters came to a head in 1816: Dundas's 30-year rule as governor came to an end when he was ousted by Kirkman Finlay, who was head of the largest firm in the Scottish cotton trade and pre-eminent in Glasgow civic life.[56]

Steam Dredgers

The first successful use, on a continuing basis, of the steam engine afloat was not as a propelling mechanism, but to power the machinery of dredgers. The first steam dredger was put into use in 1798 in Sunderland harbour on the River Wear. It was a 'bag-and-spoon' dredger, an old-established type in which a winch raised a large scoop from the river bed: in this case traditional manpower for the winch was replaced by a Boulton & Watt steam engine.[57] A more advanced pattern of dredger was the 'bucket ladder' type, in which mud was raised by an endless chain of buckets. By the end of the eighteenth century such dredgers, powered by horses, were in use. Subsequent steam dredgers were of this type.

The first to be built was proposed by Sir Samuel Bentham, Director General of Naval Works, to the Admiralty in 1800, and built at Portsmouth during 1800–1802 under the superintendence of Simon Goodrich, Bentham's assistant, described as his 'mechanist'. It may have incorporated the engine, or parts of it, from Lord Stanhope's 'ambi-navigator' *Kent*, which had been paid for from public funds and was still in store. The dredger was given extensive trials at Portsmouth, pronounced satisfactory in 1803, and set to work on a regular basis clearing shoals and deepening channels in Portsmouth Harbour, which it did satisfactorily for many years. A second dredger was ordered, and built at Deptford. It would have incorporated a Trevithick high-pressure engine, had this action not been discouraged by the explosion of the cast iron boiler of one of these at nearby Greenwich. A low-pressure boiler and engine were fitted instead, and it went into use at Woolwich in 1807.[58]

Oliver Evans was an American pioneer of high-pressure steam. He was a resident of Philadelphia and in touch with Fitch. From the mid-1780s he was proposing use of steam power for propulsion on land and water but was unable to make practical progress, largely from lack of funds. In 1802 he was commissioned to provide the steam engine for an 80-foot boat to be assembled at New Orleans for use on the Mississippi. By the time the engine arrived there in 1803, however, the hull had been swept away by a spring flood, damaged and deposited half-a-mile from the water. The engine was used in a sawmill.

Evans's chance came in 1804 when he was commissioned by the Philadelphia Board of Health to build a steam dredger for the docks. This was a lighter 30 feet long and 12 feet beam into which he fitted a 5 hp steam engine and a chain of buckets, and he built it, Noah's Ark-like, at his works one and a half miles from the water. With the practical problems of moving boats over land doubtless fresh in his mind from New Orleans, he nevertheless saw this as a fine opportunity to demonstrate the potential of his steam engine for propelling both vehicles and vessels. First the completed *Orukter Amphibolos* (the meaning of which is, apparently, 'amphibious digger') was fitted with temporary wheels, to which the engine was connected, and driven through the streets of Philadelphia. At the water's edge the wheels were removed, the vessel launched, and a stern paddle wheel fitted and connected to the engine. It was then successfully navigated on the water. Despite this convincing demonstration of steam propulsion, however, no backers emerged to fund further development. *Orukter Amphibolos* was set to its intended task of dredging the river.[59]

Back in the UK, late in 1804 the proposal was made to use a steam dredger during construction of the Caledonian Canal. Since the story of this canal is inextricably bound up with the introduction of steamboats, it is necessary to enlarge upon it. The Caledonian Canal, which was authorised in 1803, was the greatest engineering project of the age: a waterway from coast to coast, through the Great Glen from Fort William to Inverness or, to be precise, from Loch Linnhe to the Beauly Firth, incorporating the freshwater lochs Loch Lochy, Loch Oich and Loch Ness into its course and linking them with lengths of wide canal.

The waterway's purposes were twofold. Firstly, while it was being built it was to relieve hardship in the Highlands by providing home-based employment and reducing the incentive to emigrate at a time when the population was growing but changing agriculture was supporting fewer people. Secondly, once complete, it was to provide a route from coast to coast which would enable ships (sailing ships, for there were no others in 1803) to avoid the perilous voyage round the north of Scotland.[60] Regarded as a work of national importance, the Caledonian Canal was administered by commissioners appointed by Parliament, under the chairmanship of the speaker of the House of Commons, and engineered by the most notable engineers of the day – William Jessop (1745–1814) and Thomas Telford (1757–1834) in the early stages, Telford alone in the later ones.

The Caledonian Canal was intended particularly for warships, and for ships bringing timber from the Baltic to the west coast of England, and its engineering works were on a scale to suit. The flight of eight connected locks at Banavie, which became known as 'Neptune's Staircase', alone required a masonry structure some 45 feet wide and no less than 500 yards long.[61] Building such a waterway even today would be a huge undertaking: building it two centuries ago was a colossal one. And paradoxically, this project conceived during the days of sail could not have been brought to completion without the use of steam power.

Firstly, steam power was needed in the form of pumps to keep the workings clear of water – particularly where the chambers were being excavated for the locks by which the canal entered the sea or the freshwater lochs. The masonry for such locks had to extend well below the water level, and to be built behind coffer dams past which inevitably there was leakage.

Secondly, in a long report to the commissioners dated 29 November 1804, Jessop and Telford advised them:

For deepening Loch Oich and Doughfour Loch[62] we think it adviseable to construct a Machine similar to those used at Hull and Yarmouth, except that instead of working it by Horses, which from the scarcity of provender in this country would be expensive, we think it much better to work by means of a small Steam Engine; and as its operation will be slow, compared with the Work it will have to perform, it appears advisable to prepare and set it to work in the course of the next year.[63]

This advice was heeded. The components for a 6 hp steam engine were built to Jessop's design at Butterley Ironworks, Derbyshire – they cost £430 10s – during 1805 and shipped north together with the machinery for a bucket-ladder dredger. The barge in which they were to be mounted, which cost just over £456, was built at Inverness. All of them were then moved from Inverness to Loch Oich, probably by land to the foot of Loch Ness, then by water up the loch to Fort Augustus, and then overland again to Loch Oich. Despite the presence of the military road, this can have been no small undertaking, and perhaps explains why the barge had to be re-framed at the loch side.[64] Butterley's engine erector then spent thirty-three weeks setting up the engine and dredging machinery on board.[65]

But after all this expense and effort the dredger never went into service. Rather, Telford wrote on 15 October 1806 to John Rickman, secretary to the commissioners, about it:

Just as it was compleated and two or three days before we set out to the westward, owing to some of the caulking of the barge giving way, it sunk in from about 24 to 26 feet of water, leaving only (in the present state of the water) some small parts of the Timber framing above water. But as the Loch, in dry weather, sinks about five feet below this level, it will then be only in about 19 to 21 feet of water.

As we at present cannot afford to form an establishment here, and I now forsee that there will be little difficulty in deepening what is necessary in this Lock [sic, but Loch is doubtless intended] during the time the Canal is cutting between it and Fort Augustus to the East, and Loch Lochy to the West, I consider this circumstance of the Barge and Dredging Machine sinking as rather a favourable circumstance. It is just in a depth of water sufficient to cover and protect the work, without any expense of attendance and when it is prudent to begin to excavate, the whole may be then raised by means of two Barges which must be provided to carry away the Mud and Gravel. I mention these circumstances more particularly at present because persons who are not aware of the general scheme consider this as a misfortune.[66]

This startling piece of writing seems almost more remarkable for what it omits than what it says. The full circumstances behind Telford's strange action, or rather inaction, can only be guessed at. It does appear that the dredger was very much Jessop's concept, and the relationship between Telford and Jessop was ever a delicate one.[67]

More remarkably still, the dredger was not raised when dredging operations did eventually start in Loch Oich in 1817: an entirely new vessel, of more advanced design, was used instead. The existence of the earlier dredger seems, from that point on, to have been air-brushed out of history.

It would be interesting to know if it still lies where it sank and, if so, whether it would be practicable to recover all or any of it. Recovery of an unused steam engine built in 1805 would be a triumph. But it may well have been removed discretely long since, as a hazard to navigation perhaps, or simply for scrap.

Use of a steam dredger to improve the tidal River Orwell below Ipswich was proposed as early as 1797 in a report by the engineer William Chapman (1749–1832). Chapman knew both William Jessop and James Watt; he had early experience of steam engines but spent most of his career as a civil engineer on canal and land drainage works. This particular proposal lay fallow until 1805 when an Act of Parliament authorised the work: Chapman immediately ordered a steam dredger with a Boulton, Watt & Co. engine and Butterley dredging machinery. It started work in 1806 and continued in service until 1839.[68] Richard Trevithick did eventually have dredgers powered by his high-pressure steam engines at work in the Thames tideway in 1806–7.[69] From this time on, use of steam dredgers became increasingly common. The Caledonian Canal had a steam dredger at work at Loch Dochfour from November 1814,[70] and a second one was built in 1816 with two bucket ladders, one each side, for Loch Oich.[71]

Fulton in France, and in Britain Again

A republican by nature and by conviction, Robert Fulton probably felt more at home in the France of the late 1790s than in England.[72] Having arrived in Paris in 1797, he took up residence in the home of Joel Barlow. Barlow was a prominent, cultured and wealthy American resident, although the source of that wealth was a mystery – perhaps running goods across frontiers closed by war. Fulton stayed with Barlow and his wife Ruth for the next seven years or so, forming it seems a sort of *ménage à trois*. On this subject, however fascinating it might be, there is no space to enlarge here. It is peripheral to the main theme. So, more regrettably, is the next of Fulton's important activities. He had gone to France apparently to promote his ideas on canals. He found himself building a submarine.

Such a vessel had been built a couple of decades earlier by David Bushnell and used against the British fleet in New York harbour in 1776; Bushnell and his work were probably known to Barlow. Fulton, however, had apparently to discover the details again from first principles. His intention, like Bushnell's, was to use the submarine to place what he called 'torpedoes', and what we would think of, since they were not self-propelled, as 'mines', beneath naval ships: those of the British navy, to blow them up. This seems a distinctly unfriendly act, given the welcome he had until recently been enjoying in England. Fulton seems to have justified it to himself by a belief that destruction of all navies would lead to free trade and peace on earth. There was also the prospect of big financial reward from the French government. Astonishingly, Fulton achieved a high degree of technical success, building a vessel which sailed on the surface, dived, and when beneath the surface was propelled by the muscle power of the occupants; the torpedoes, too, were successful on test. An attempt to blow up two British brigs off the Normandy coast failed when, forewarned, they set sail at his approach. Fulton's work on canals had demonstrated his ability to assimilate the work of predecessors: his work on the submarine demonstrated his ability to put assimilated knowledge successfully to practical use, and at some personal danger too.

Fulton's interest in steamboats seems to have been re-kindled by the arrival in Paris in 1801 of Robert Livingston as Minister Plenipotentiary of the United States to France. Two years later Livingston would negotiate the Louisiana Purchase – the purchase of much of the Mid-West of America from France by the United States, opening up New Orleans and the Mississippi River as a trade route to and from American settlements already in existence to the north – with all that that would imply for the development of the steamboat. That, however, is to leap far ahead. Before leaving for France Livingston had obtained from the State of New York the exclusive privilege of operating steamboats within that state, provided he built such a boat, to go at 4 mph, within a year. He had been in touch with Boulton & Watt. The powers had lapsed, but were later renewed. Quite soon after his arrival in Paris, Fulton was introduced to him, and the two started to make plans.

Fulton studied the theory of hull shapes[73] – long and narrow for a steamboat, he concluded – he considered the work of predecessors, and he carried out trials with a spring-driven model to establish the best mode of propulsion. As a result of these he favoured an endless chain of floatboards; then he moved to paddle wheels, probably in response to a French patent recently taken out by a rival, whose work came eventually to nothing. The trials were done in the late spring of 1802 on a dammed-up stream at Plombières, a spa in eastern France, to which he had accompanied Ruth Barlow for the summer. Joel Barlow meanwhile looked after Fulton's interests in Paris, while Livingston with many other preoccupations blew hot and cold on the project.

On 26 July 1802 Barlow wrote to Fulton proposing that he should go to England 'silent and steady' to arrange for William Chapman, whom he had just visited, to build a steam engine, and offering to find the funds for this 'without any noise'.[74] This was the time of the Peace of Amiens, when hostilities between France and Britain had ceased (as it turned out, only temporarily), and travel between the two countries was comparatively easy. It has long been the author's opinion that Fulton probably did pay a brief visit to Britain at this time, clandestinely, for in view of his recent anti-British activities he could scarcely have travelled under his own name, and he would soon demonstrate an aptitude for travel incognito. He may have visited Chapman; he probably did go north and inspect the first *Charlotte Dundas*. Robert Weir, her fireman, would later state in a sworn affidavit:

> That, some time after the first experiment, while the boat was lying upon the canal at Lock 16, it was visited by a stranger, who requested to see the boat worked. That the said William Symington desired the deponent to light the furnace, which was done, and the stranger was carried about four miles along the canal, and brought back. That this stranger made inquiries both as to the mode of construction and of working the boat, and took notes of the information given him by the said William Symington. That the deponent heard the stranger say his name was Fulton [in these circumstances, so far from the seat of power in London, Fulton might well have thought it safe, indeed preferable, to use his own name], and that he was a native of the United States of America. That the deponent remembers Mr Symington remarking that the progress of the boat was much impeded by the narrowness of the canal, to which Mr Fulton answered that the objection would not apply to the large rivers of North America, where he thought the boat might be used to great advantage.[75]

The problem is that all the evidence for this visit seems to come from Symington sources, and little if any from Fulton sources: these suggest that Fulton was at Plombières for the entire summer. Many other dates have been suggested for it.[76] Yet Fulton's absence from Paris at another time would have been remarked upon; absence for two or three weeks from Plombières would have been far less conspicuous.

Fulton and Ruth Barlow did, however, arrive back in Paris that September. On 10 October Fulton and Livingston reached a formal agreement. They would build a steamboat to carry sixty passengers between New York and Albany (on the Hudson River), and Fulton would take out a US patent for a new mechanical combination of a boat to navigate by the power of a steam engine. But first, they agreed, Fulton would go to England to build an experimental boat and the cost would be underwritten by Livingston. Livingston had his New York State steamboat privilege, which had lapsed again, renewed in their joint names.

In fact, the experimental boat was built at Paris, that winter. After a first version sank, a second was built. The engine and transmission incorporated, for marine use, an important advance. The heavy overhead beam was eliminated. Instead, the piston rod terminated at a crosshead from which connecting rods led downwards, either side of the cylinder, to bell cranks located low in the boat. From the further ends of these, linked together across the boat, another connecting rod led to the crank on the paddle-wheel shaft.[77] The centre of gravity of the whole was lowered a lot, the stability of the boat greatly increased.

After private trials, Fulton demonstrated the boat in public, on the Seine at Paris, in August 1803. He towed two other boats up and down the river, manoeuvred with them, came up to anchor and set off again, all without problems. Watching crowds were delighted. It was a success as complete as that of Symington with the second *Charlotte Dundas* five months before, and it would have much greater consequences.

Even before the public trial, Fulton had sent to Boulton, Watt & Co. a detailed enquiry for steam engine components, to be shipped when complete to New York. By October, however, Boulton, Watt & Co. had been unable to obtain permission to export them, and politely declined the order. But times were changing. War had broken out again between Britain and France – Fulton's letters to Boulton, Watt & Co. had had to be routed via Hamburg and sent in triplicate in the hope that one copy might arrive. Napoleon's forces were massing in northern France for his proposed invasion. As early as 1802 Lord Stanhope had warned the House of Lords, in a dramatic intervention for which the public galleries were cleared, of the threat presented by Fulton's submarine activities. There was good reason for the British authorities to want Fulton on their side rather than that of France. By late 1803 a British agent, 'Mr Smith', had approached him. The approach was by no means unwelcome to Fulton. A republican idealist, he was observing the regime in France becoming less and less democratic. It had become clear too that the French authorities, despite a direct approach to Napoleon, were not going to take up the submarine or the torpedoes. By May 1804 'Robert Francis', alias Fulton, was on his way to England.

There was a delay in London while the British government set up a commission to consider the merits of Fulton's submarine and torpedoes. Its distinguished members included John Rennie. Then Fulton set out for Birmingham to order a steam engine from Boulton, Watt & Co. James Watt had been retired for some years, and the firm was in the hands of the younger generation. Fulton found it much more receptive to an order for a steamboat engine than it had been previously – particularly, it seems, from someone who called in person, knew exactly what he wanted, and had practical experience to his credit. He may also have found a kindred spirit in James Watt Jr, who as a young man had favoured the French Revolution and had taken part in the revolutionary movement in Paris between 1792 and 1794, to the extent of being denounced in the House of Commons as a traitor.[78]

By mid-July Fulton had ordered the metal components for a bell-crank steam engine – a cylinder of 24-inch diameter by 48-inch stroke, piston, piston rod, valve gear, condenser, air pump, pipework and other lesser parts – all for a quoted price of £380. Some amicable correspondence followed about modifications to the original plans. One in particular concerned the air pump – the pump which extracts condensate and air from the condenser – which, since it was to be exposed to salt water, was to be made of brass rather than iron. This brought the total price up to £548 consequent upon, wrote Boulton, Watt & Co., 'the advanced price of copper'. The whole was despatched to Fulton in London by canal boat in February 1805 after some delay, it seems, because the canal had been frozen over. Fulton then obtained permission for export from the Treasury, and shipped it off to New York.[79] He may have had a copper boiler made in London, or he may have obtained one later in America: authorities, as so often, differ.

Eventually, he returned to America himself. Earlier, to his chagrin, he had learned that the British naval authorities had declined to adopt his submarine, but were interested in developing the torpedoes which, they felt, could be delivered with much less trouble by surface vessels. Months of trials, largely inconclusive, and expeditions against the French, partly successful, had followed. Eventually the victory at Trafalgar in 1805 removed the threat from the French navy, and British naval interest in the torpedoes evaporated.

But in the meantime Fulton had been paid a high salary, which must have helped with the advanced price of copper. Fulton finally arrived back in America in December 1806.

Fulton's Success, and Successors

Fulton's steamboat was built at New York in the spring of 1807, 133 feet long, 13-foot beam, and 2-foot draught. The engine was built up and fitted and the boiler, externally fired, was installed. On 10 August Fulton was able to write to Robert Livingston, who was back home again, that he had the previous day carried out what amounted to a preliminary trial which indicated that the boat would, when complete, meet expectations, and that she handled well. Modifications and improvements followed, and presumably some more discrete trial runs – for without these the first public trial, commencing on 17 August, would have been exceptionally ambitious. With Fulton and forty of his friends and relatives aboard, the steamboat set out up the Hudson River at 1.00 p.m. for Clermont, Livingston's residence 110 miles to the north. She reached it 24 hours later. After an overnight stay, she set off again, with Livingston now aboard, at 9.00 a.m. for Albany, 40 miles further on, reached at 5.00 p.m. The southbound journey was run in similar times, with a halt of one hour only at Clermont. There was a head wind the whole time, northbound and southbound. The machinery, according to one of the passengers, moved 'with all the facility of a clock'.[80]

After this amazing performance a fortnight or so was spent on final details and on 4 September the *North River Steamboat* went into service carrying passengers between New York and Albany, which she continued to do, without any fundamental faults emerging, until the river started to freeze over in November. Nevertheless she was much rebuilt over the winter before going back into service the following spring.[81] In due course she acquired the name *Clermont* by which she has been famous ever since.

Clermont became the first of some seventeen steamboats which Fulton designed or built over the next decade. Many of them were operated on the Hudson. And once he had shown the way, he was not alone. In 1802–3 John Stevens, who was married to Livingston's sister, had built two small steamboats, screw-driven and with high pressure boilers which had shown great promise. In the spring of 1808 he built a much larger steamboat, the *Phoenix*, with a view to operating her commercially on the Hudson. This produced a war of words between the brothers-in-law on the subject of monopolies, with the upshot that in the summer of 1809 Stevens decided to move his boat to the Delaware River. That meant 150 miles of open water, making *Phoenix* the first steamboat to go to sea, although she seems to have headed for shelter at the first sign of trouble and took thirteen days for the voyage. She subsequently operated between Philadelphia and Trenton.[82]

So the next steamboat to go into public service, after the *Clermont*, was the *Vermont* on Lake Champlain, the 120-mile-long lake on the borders of Vermont, the state of New York and the province of Quebec. Coincidentally, it had three decades before been the scene of naval actions in which Captain Schank had played a prominent part.[83] The *Vermont* was built by the brothers John and James Winans, both of whom had worked for Fulton, at Burlington, Vermont. She was 128 feet long by 20 feet beam with a 20 hp engine, and cost $20,000. She went into service on the lake in June 1809, operating out of Basin Harbor, and became the first of many steamers to operate on Lake Champlain over the next 140 years.[84]

The *Vermont* had been influenced in her layout by that of Fulton's *Clermont*, and so was that of the first steamboat in Canada, the *Accommodation* built at Montreal with a locally-made engine in 1809 for the brewer John Molson, who had originated in Lincolnshire. She operated on the St Lawrence between Montreal and Quebec but proved underpowered, and for his next boat Molson ordered an engine from Boulton, Watt & Co. in 1811. This was the third marine engine they built, for they had already supplied a second engine to Fulton. On test, Molson's second boat, *Swiftsure*, achieved 9 mph downstream and 5.3 mph up, which was evidently considered satisfactory, for Molson returned to Boulton, Watt & Co. for his next steamboat engine four years later.[85]

The steamboat finally reached the Mississippi, of which Fulton and Livingston had long entertained great hopes, in the form of the *New Orleans*, built at Pittsburgh by Nicholas Roosevelt to plans supplied by Fulton. She was launched in 1811 and after a perilous 2,000-mile journey down the Ohio and Mississippi Rivers reached New Orleans in January 1812, after which she plied between New Orleans and Natchez.[86]

Wherever a steamboat was put into service, others soon followed. In the New World, that is. The Old World was asleep. Steamboat experiments were a tale of promises unfulfilled. Probably people had wearied of the subject. In London, particularly, successive experiments by Stanhope and Rumsey had led nowhere.

Joseph Chessborough Dyer, an American, arrived in London in 1811. Dyer was making a business of acting on behalf of American inventors to promote their inventions in Britain, where he would eventually settle. He had personal experience of travel on the *Clermont*. He brought with him full descriptions and drawings of Fulton's steamboat discoveries, with the aim of persuading British engineers and men of capital to take them up. He could arouse no interest. Compared with America, he was told, rivers were small and harbours crowded. Steamboats would not do. Even John Rennie was discouraging.[87]

Neither of them can have known that Henry Bell, who had been growing up and establishing himself in business throughout most of the period covered by the events described in this chapter, was already making plans to build a steamboat.

THREE

Henry Bell Himself

The village of Torphichen lies in the central belt of Scotland, closer to the east coast than the west, deep in the green hinterland of West Lothian. Linlithgow is a few miles to the north, Bathgate a couple of miles to the south. Torphichen was perhaps better known in the Middle Ages than today: here the Order of St John of Jerusalem – the Knights Hospitallers – established its preceptory, or headquarters, in Scotland. Part of the building survives as the parish church, part survives in ruins.

Torphichen village lies high up, so its water mill was located a mile or so to the north-west, down in the deep and winding valley of the River Avon. This flows northwards towards Linthithgow and eventually reaches the Firth of Forth. Torphichen mill was one of many which this river formerly powered, and in the late 1760s the miller was Patrick Bell, who was married to Margaret Easton, daughter of John Easton of Stirlingshire. The Bell family had long been resident in this part of Scotland. Some of its members were famous as millwrights as well as millers; members of the Easton family were if anything more so. Patrick and Margaret Bell's fifth son, Henry, was born at Torphichen Mill on 7 April 1767. Or maybe it was 7 April 1768 – there is uncertainty here, as in so much of Henry Bell's later activities. In due course he was baptised at Bathgate.[1]

The eighteenth-century millwright required the knowledge and skills of what we would now call a civil engineer to construct and maintain mill lades, dams and the like; and he required the knowledge and skills of the mechanical engineer to build and maintain milling machinery. By that date, too, water power had moved on from simply powering corn mills to powering the factories of the early Industrial Revolution. It was from the ranks of millwrights that there sprang many of those who would soon become well known as engineers – as has been hinted at in chapter one in the brief résumé of John Rennie's early career. Two of the contractors for the Forth & Clyde Canal, the main part of which, from Grangemouth to near Glasgow, was built between 1768 and 1775, came from the Easton family. They were father (John, probably) and son, Alexander. In the next generation Alexander's son, also called Alexander Easton (1787–1854), would become well-known as one of the great Thomas Telford's right-hand men. In 1807, at the early age of twenty, he was appointed by Telford as resident engineer for construction of the western division of the Caledonian Canal, and he continued in that position until it was opened in 1822.[2] The precise degree of relationship between this branch of the Easton family and Margaret Bell, née Easton, remains despite research uncertain – but they all certainly came from the same part of Scotland. Alexander Easton was born near Carron Ironworks and baptised, as Henry Bell had been, at Bathgate. The link is noteworthy, however, in view of the important role that Bell would eventually play in developing traffic through the Caledonian Canal, described in chapter seven.

All that, however, lay far in the future, for a small boy growing up at Torphichen Mill where the surging sounds of the watercourse blended with the soothing rumble of the mill machinery. He attended the parish school, and then from the ages of nine to twelve he was sent to stay with Easton relations in Falkirk to attend the school there, where the teaching of mathematics was better. From 1783 to 1786 he worked with a relative as a stone mason, and then he was apprenticed for three years to a Bell uncle as a millwright.[3]

In 1786, at the age of eighteen or nineteen, he made what appears as a sideways move, going to work for shipbuilders Shaw & Hart at Bo'ness – or Borrowstounness, to give it its full name. Bo'ness lies on the shore of the Forth about six miles north of Torphichen and was then, and despite the challenge of newly-established Grangemouth, one of the most important ports of the east of Scotland. Shaw & Hart was one of two shipbuilders established there, and with them Bell spent a year gaining experience in ship design and construction.[4]

In 1787 he moved to an engineer near Glasgow for a time, and after that to London, for about eighteen months, to John Rennie. At this period Rennie's work on the Albion Mills was approaching completion; he was building up a wider engineering consultancy, particularly in relation to use of steam engines, and also embarking on canal engineering. This would all be valuable experience for Bell, but unfortunately we do not know in what capacity Rennie employed him. Nor do we know precise dates. What Bell later told his nineteenth-century biographer Edward Morris was, 'I went to London, to the famous Mr Rennie, which shows I was not a self-taught engineer, as some of my friends have supposed.'[5] Further, his twentieth-century biographer Brian Osborne notes that there do not appear to be any references to Bell in what he describes as 'Rennie's voluminous papers'.[6] So it seems unlikely that Bell's position was a senior one: if it had been, he would scarcely have resisted the temptation to tell the world about it. But doubtless it was none the less beneficial.

At any rate the culmination of this worthy programme of education and self-improvement was that in 1790 he was back in Scotland, not in the district of his origins but in Glasgow, where the following year he entered into a partnership with a James Paterson, as Bell & Paterson, builders.[7]

Glasgow then was a town growing rapidly in population, in importance, and in prosperity. A population of 23,546 in 1755 had grown to 42,832 in 1780, and would continue to expand rapidly to 110,460 in 1811, 147,043 in 1821 and about 170,000 in 1825.[8] Earlier dependence on the tobacco trade had been replaced by manufacture of consumer goods – boots, glass, soap, candles, pottery and much else, but particularly textiles, notably cotton.[9] The first steam engine erected in Glasgow, for spinning cotton, was put up in January 1792.[10] Such a place clearly offered much to attract a young man setting up in the building trade.

At this point it is necessary to pause, briefly, in this chronological account of Henry Bell's career, and to consider his character and characteristics. Something of the complexity of his character has already been mentioned in chapter one, and more can be discerned in his relationship with Rennie, mentioned above. However, as his appearance suggests – portraits show penetrating blue eyes set in a large honest face – he evidently had a great deal of charm, and the ability to get on with anybody at a personal level. Biographer Edward Morris, who knew him well, recalled his good-natured smile, his witty, innocent anecdotes.[11] But others who knew him well recalled also his restless, ingenious, unmethodical mind.[12] Contemporaries often saw him as a 'schemer', although not in the pejorative sense. He became, rather, a visionary whose great ideas ran ahead of his ability to bring them to fruition. Although not by very much.

There was, of course, a down side. Bell was carefree in his attitude to money. More seriously, he had great difficulty in expressing himself in writing. What he did write was rendered scarcely intelligible, to the reader, by inaccurate spelling and unconventional grammar. He was not alone in this among his peers. James Brindley, millwright turned famous canal engineer, would commence operations with an 'ochilor servey or ricconitoring'. Richard Trevithick's spelling was idiosyncratic. George Stephenson, 'father of railways', was still illiterate at the age of eighteen. He subsequently learned to read and write. Henry Bell's writings remained, as he himself put it, 'ungramatick scrals'[13] until the end of his life. Brian Osborne offers as a suitable example part of a letter written in 1820 to a potential investor in the *Comet*:

> I was favered with a letter from Mr McIntayer–informing me that you wished to have a shair in the *Comet* steam boat…this is my terms and the said £45 to be paid me just now and for surety of your I cass you to be indorsed on the back of the register and allow on the general rindishion of the *Comet* steam boat and your rights will be as good as the other partners if this is agreeable to your views pleas send me the cash.[14]

At least the meaning of the last few words is clear enough! But in general, even when allowance is made for the vagaries of early nineteenth-century spelling, Bell's manner of expressing himself was bizarre. Today he would be diagnosed as dyslexic.[15] In a world which tends to equate lack of ability to spell with lack of intelligence, or at least lack of education, such a condition was and is a huge disadvantage. But it is at least involuntary.

Another of Bell's characteristics regrettably was not entirely so. It was to become increasingly marked as he approached old age, and it may indeed have been to some extent a reaction to those who, knowing him only through the written word, tended to under-rate his abilities. This characteristic was a tendency, although his achievements were remarkable enough, to exaggerate, to claim even more. Examples will appear as the story unfolds. The consequence, unfortunately, is that every claim he made, in the press or in conversation with his biographer, and particularly when related to priority of himself or others in the introduction of steam boats, has to be treated with caution. The position is aggravated by a tendency for Morris, his biographer, to accept what Bell told him without question. This does not mean that every claim that Bell made can be discounted: there may be fantasy, but there is also often an element of truth in them. Brian Osborne summed up this characteristic delightfully as 'a tendency to a creative reinterpretation of historical evidence'[16]: it would be difficult to improve on that description.

One of the apparent consequences of this was that, even in his own time and soon after, Bell was being denigrated as for instance no more than a mere house-carpenter.[17] These contrary opinions have been carried down to recent times: from a publication of 1952, for instance, we learn that, at the time of the *Comet*, abler men than Bell had contrived to fit engines into hulls, that he had brief experience as a millwright, that he was a fantastical, sanguine party of the speculative type who eventually persuaded a respectable building firm to construct a hull, bought a steam engine and found a boiler somewhere else, and that these were somehow put together.[18] As we shall see, it was not quite like that. H. P. Spratt, authority on early steamboats, was nearer the mark when he commented that Bell was not an inventor or man of science, but was a man of considerable shrewdness, with a rich vein of humour, full of schemes and optimism, but without the commercial tenacity to turn his enterprise into money.[19] Indeed it does seem that in the late stages of his life, although Bell was ambitious, his motivation was to improve things for the general good rather than to accumulate a personal fortune. Fame rather than fortune was the spur: he did want recognition.

Most of this lay in the distant future for the young man setting up in business in Glasgow in the early 1790s, although in his selection of this rapidly growing town it is possible to discern something of the way in which his mind was starting to move. Presumably booming Glasgow produced plenty of work for the partnership, which lasted until 1798, although little is known for certain at this stage in Bell's career. He was however able to join the appropriate trade guild, the Incorporation of Wrights, in 1797. His design for a church in Carluke was accepted in 1799, and at this time or soon afterwards he built a large flour mill at Partick.[20] Iron castings needed for his buildings he obtained from the foundry of John Napier[21] – a contact which would serve him well a few years later. In 1806 he published an ambitious plan for supplying the growing city with a water supply drawn from the River Clyde near Lanark. From that point water would flow by gravity down a 30-mile-long cut – an outsize mill-lade, perhaps – to Glasgow. This was a response to a proposal by Thomas Telford to improve the water supply by pumping water from the Clyde nearer the city, with a steam engine.[22] Telford's proposal was adopted, but it is noteworthy that when, decades later, Glasgow's water supply was augmented still further by drawing from Loch Katrine, the method used was essentially the same as that which Bell had proposed.

Henry Bell's private life had moved forward when in 1794 he married Margaret Young. He chose well: she was a person in whom cheerfulness was blended with common sense, who would as time went by act as a counterweight to her husband's extreme enthusiasms. She was also good at managing money.

After some years in a town which was old-established but growing fast, Bell's next move was to one which was of recent foundation and still far short of reaching its full potential. To a man of his inclinations, this must have seemed an attractive proposition.

Sir James Colquhoun of Luss had decided to found a new village on his land on the north shore of the Firth of Clyde in the 1770s, with the intention of attracting weavers, bonnet makers and the like. He started to offer feus, or long leases, of land for houses in 1776, and about 1785 the village was named Helensburgh in honour of his wife. But there were not many takers for the feus, and by the 1790s Helensburgh had only around 100 inhabitants.[23] To encourage its growth it received a royal charter in 1802 establishing it as a Burgh of Barony with a heraldic crest, the right to hold weekly markets and four annual fairs, and to administer itself, for which purpose there were to be a provost, two baillies and four councillors[24] elected by the feuars. And here, in 1806, Henry Bell feued a piece of land adjoining the shore,[25] and started to build the Baths Inn.

In building a 'baths inn' Bell, in character, was seeking to turn to advantage a trend of the time, one of rapidly increasing popularity. Sea-bathing, for its health benefits, first became popular in the second half of the eighteenth century. It was allied to the practice of taking the waters at inland spas, old-established but likewise of rapidly increasing popularity. Sea-bathing was recommended by the medical profession specifically for skin complaints, and generally for maintaining good health. King George III gave the practice royal approval by bathing in the sea at Weymouth in 1789. Margate had already become a fashionable watering place around 1760. In Scotland, Peterhead had a salt-water bath, in addition to mineral springs, as early as 1762. Portobello, close to Edinburgh, had bathing machines by 1795. Gourock was popular for sea-bathing by the early 1790s, and the practice of moving one's family to the coast in summer was already emerging. Sea-bathing resorts, and inland spas, needed accommodation for their visitors – Lord Hopetoun, for instance, had built two inns in Moffat as early as the 1760s with a view to attracting visitors to this spa town.[26] Across the Clyde from Gourock, the new village of Helensburgh too was getting a reputation for sea-bathing in the 1790s[27] – its beaches then and for long afterwards were sandy – and here in about 1807 Henry and Margaret Bell opened the Baths Inn to the public.[28]

The Baths Inn soon became a well-known and familiar feature of Helensburgh, a whitewashed, four-square castellated building standing out upon the foreshore. Managed mostly by Margaret Bell, it acquired a reputation for good hospitality, and as well as all the usual accommodation for visitors there were in due course a heated conservatory and an extensive range of hot and cold baths for invalids.[29] To pump seawater into the baths there were a steam engine and/or a waterwheel driven pump – authorities vary on this. In the present author's opinion there are quite likely to have been both, used as alternatives: the steam engine would have been the more expensive to run, but the more reliable in times of water shortage such as the summer when most visitors, presumably, arrived. The engine was provided in 1808 by John Robertson, a young Glasgow engineer – and since he was to play a vital part in the story of the *Comet* and what came after, it is necessary to know a little more about him.

John Robertson had been born in 1782 in Neilston, Renfrewshire, where his father James (who originated from Stanley, Perthshire) was managing a cotton mill. At the age of fourteen he was apprenticed for four years to a maker of spinning-wheels, and then went to Stanley to work as a turner, probably at the cotton mills, for two years. After that he moved to Glasgow, to work, and to continue his training, with machine-maker William Dunn; and by 1808 he had become sufficiently skilled and knowledgeable to have built, in his leisure time, a small steam engine of 2 hp. This was the engine which Bell saw: he successfully bargained with Robertson to bring it to the Baths Inn and set it up – a task which Robertson is said to have executed much to Bell's satisfaction.[30] The engine was evidently still present in the 1830s.[31]

Bell's ambitions for Helensburgh ran to more than providing the town with a good hotel and bathing establishment. Until his arrival, no attempt seems to have been made to exploit the corporate powers granted to the burgh by its charter. In 1807, however, the feuars elected him the town's first provost, and elected baillies and councillors too. The new council was soon making plans to build streets and hold markets. It also proposed to build a town's house or municipal building, and Bell and one of the baillies obtained the necessary feu. In this instance, however, Bell's ambitions seem to have outstripped those of his fellow townsmen and within a few months the feu was given up. A proposal to provide the town with a piped water supply – just the sort of scheme to originate from Bell – appears to have been more successful. This particular phase in Bell's career came to an end in 1811 when he ceased to be provost. At this time he sold the Baths Inn to Archibald Newbigging, a prominent Glasgow merchant. He continued there, however, as tenant, with Margaret continuing to manage it.[32] It sounds like a sale-and-lease-back arrangement, probably made to release funds for the steamboat experiments shortly to be described.

Bell also continued to undertake other projects. After Dalmonach print works burned down around 1812, it was Bell who rebuilt them. This textile printing works dated from 1786 and stood beside the River Leven at Bonhill, some six miles east of Helensburgh as the crow flies. It was one of many textile works in the Vale of Leven using the river of that name as its source of power.[33] Clearly superintending its reconstruction was work which Bell was well equipped to undertake. Perhaps it was close acquaintanceship with the Leven at this period which caused him also to take an interest in the possibilities of improving this river for navigation and simultaneously reclaiming low-lying ground on the shores of Loch Lomond (out of which the river flows) for agriculture. This was a live issue from the 1770s through to the 1840s, without result.[34]

By this date Bell was in his mid-forties. He had evidently become a moderately successful middle-ranking businessman, although one with big ideas and an eye to getting in on the ground floor. But he would today have been forgotten long since, had it not been for his next move. This would result in his introduction of the first successful steamboat service – the first successful mechanised passenger transport – outside North America. It was prompted, however, by a more localised and specific need: the need to alleviate the difficulties of travel to the Baths Inn and his adopted home town of Helensburgh.

FOUR

The Genesis of the Comet

There were two ways by which people could travel from Glasgow to Helensburgh: by road, and by river.

Roads, originally, had been no more than traditional routes across country, tracks seldom wide enough for a vehicle on wheels, and maintained by the limited resources of the local populace. This was formalised as 'statute labour' by seventeenth-century Acts of Parliament which required the people in each parish to spend several days each year working on its roads. As time went by, many were able to commute this service for a money payment. Statute labour became invidious to residents of parishes through which main roads passed: on these long-distance traffic, increasingly on wheels, was damaging the surfaces, and to alleviate this problem it became the practice during the latter part of the eighteenth century to establish, by Act of Parliament, turnpike trusts. Trustees, drawn usually from local landowners, were enabled to set up toll-gates, and required to devote the toll revenue to maintenance and improvement of the road concerned. Such roads were well suited to the horse-drawn coaches, carts and waggons which were coming more and more into use over the same period.

In the district where Helensburgh came to be located, roads were probably rather better than usual because of the interest of the Dukes of Argyle in having good communications with their residences at Rosneath and Inveraray. Then, under a Turnpike Act of 1807, trustees were appointed for 'surveying, altering, making, maintaining, repairing and keeping in Repair the ... Roads and Bridges, leading from the west End of the Bridge of *Dumbarton* along the River *Clyde*, *Gareloch*, and *Lochlong*, to a Place called

New Tarbet'.[1] (New Tarbet was, at this date, the name of a landowner's residence just south of Arrochar.) In other words, the road to and through Helensburgh was to be turnpiked and improved.

So buying land in Helensburgh in 1806 would have been a good speculation. It may well be that Henry Bell knew that these improvements in communications were likely, and that this was a factor influencing him to move there and set up the Baths Inn at just this time. At any rate before long he was operating a coach between Helensburgh and Glasgow. Decades later, it would be remembered as a queer, rickety thing, but that was in retrospect, viewed from a world in which people had become accustomed to easy, fast travel by train or steamer.[2] In its day it must have required of Bell a considerable feat of organisation. For a driver there was his brother Thomas, who must somewhere have acquired the skills to drive horses, probably four-in-hand. The total distance, 22 miles, was too great to be covered in one stage: Bell must have arranged for fresh horses to be available not only at Helensburgh and Glasgow, but also for a change of horses to be available en route, every time the coach passed in each direction. The change was probably made at the Bowling Inn, where the coach stopped for one hour for refreshments. The total journey time was 6 hours, which allowing for the refreshment break meant an average speed of just under 4½ miles per hour: slow even by the standards of the time, for a crack coach on a good road could double that. Maybe the turnpike trustees' improvements were slow to take effect. For those who could not afford the fares of seven shillings inside, five shillings and sixpence outside, there was always the carrier's waggon – cheaper and slower still, but nevertheless preferred by some to a boat on the river, for it neither made you sick nor got stranded on sandbanks.[3]

From that it is clear that river travel had its problems too. Yet the Clyde had been used as a route for travel since pre-history, as the logboats unearthed on its shores have from time to time confirmed. Today, however, the Clyde from Greenock up to Glasgow is unusual (though not unique) in that, although tidal, it is largely an artificial waterway. Because of the central role the river was to play in the story of the first steamboats, it is necessary to consider its history in some detail and particularly its condition in the early nineteenth century. Its problems arose from its topography. From the open sea up as far as Greenock, the Firth of Clyde and the lochs which branch from it have the character of Highland sea lochs – deep, but largely sheltered and free from hazards to shipping. Then, at the Tail of the Bank, the Clyde shallows abruptly. Further up, the tidal River Clyde had originally all the character of a Lowland estuary, winding its way between low banks, full of shoals and shallows where silt washed down from upstream had been deposited. The position was exacerbated because the bed of the river was formed of harder material than the banks. So when it was in flood, the extra flow did not deepen the bed: rather it washed away the banks, rendering the river wider and, once the flood had subsided, shallower than ever.

Since sea-going ships could not reach Glasgow, the seventeenth-century solution had been to tranship goods at down-river harbours, and to use lighters or packhorses between these places and Glasgow town. Port Glasgow had been established for this purpose in the 1670s. In the eighteenth century attention had turned to the possibility of deepening the river itself. At this period the usual method of improving a river for navigation was to build weirs to maintain the depth, with locks alongside them for boats to pass. This was considered for the Clyde and supported by the noted engineer John Smeaton when Glasgow town council called him in to advise. Smeaton found a depth of no more than 15 inches at low tide in the river off Govan, and several other places where it was no more than 18 inches. He recommended a dam and lock at a location about 4 miles below Glasgow Bridge. In 1759 the council obtained an Act of Parliament to authorise these, and work started the following year. But it was never completed. The subsoil, it turned out, was not strong enough to support a large masonry structure, and after a lot of money had been spent without benefit, and no more could be raised, work was abandoned.

Successful improvement of the river eventually came about following the council's employment of John Golborne to examine and report. Golborne, a native of Chester, had experience of improving the River Dee and other waterways in that region. His solution, presented in a report of 1768, was in essence audaciously simple: by reducing the effective width of the river, to increase its flow and enable it to scour out its own bed. The means to reduce the width was to build successive dykes, or jetties, from the banks out into the river, more or less opposite one another and with only narrow openings between them. This would be supplemented by dredging where necessary. The council obtained another Act of Parliament in 1770, which appointed the Lord Provost, magistrates and councillors as statutory trustees for the Clyde, with powers to carry out the works now considered needed. Golborne was put in charge and his methods were so successful that within two years there was a location near Glasgow where at low tide the depth was 4 feet where previously it had been 15 inches. Other shoals downstream proved more recalcitrant, but methods were evolved to deal with them. At Dumbuck, 12 miles below Glasgow, where it had been possible to ford the river on foot at low tide, the main flow divided either side of an extensive shoal: a longitudinal dyke diverted the flow entirely to one side only, with the desired effect. Elsewhere, large dredging scoops of wood and iron were wound by cable laboriously across the river bed, removing a hard crust to expose softer material more easily eroded by the flow. In December 1775 a survey of the river showed that there was, as Golborne had promised, at high tide at least 7 feet depth throughout.

The work continued, with refinements, to make the river deeper still. After Golborne's death Rennie was consulted, and Telford. By 1809, even at low water, there was a depth of more than 4 feet throughout most of the channel. Instead of transhipping their cargoes downstream, ships engaged in coastal and estuary trade came right up river to Glasgow – 2,000 of them in 1810 – and small ships engaged in foreign trade were able to do likewise.[4] This was the position at the beginning of the steamboat era – subsequent deepening works throughout the nineteenth century would enable the largest ships to visit Glasgow and, particularly, to be built on the banks of the Clyde.

For passengers up and down the river, in the late eighteenth and early nineteenth century, there were fly boats, propelled by oars or sails or, in the upper reaches, towed by a horse – a horse-towing path had been one of Telford's recommendations. 'Fly' implied quick – fly boats on English canals were boats carrying merchandise and parcels with priority over slow-moving boats carrying coal and the like. On the Clyde fly boats were probably quick only in relation to lighters, which in times of low water could be detained for weeks – fly boats could measure journey times in hours, but were dependent on favourable weather and slower than coaches on land. Traditionally, passengers travelled under a canvas shelter near the stern, with the oarsmen forward of them.

The noted traveller Thomas Pennant took a boat down the river from Glasgow in 1772. After four miles he was able to call on John Golborne at his house on the north bank 'commanding a most elegant view of the county of Renfrew on the opposite bank'. The men were old friends: both came from the same part of the world. Pennant observed the dredging scoops at work, bringing up half a ton of gravel at a time. He then continued down the river, approving of the scene: 'the expanse is wide and gentle; the one bank bare, the other adorned with a small open grove. A little isle tufted with trees divides the water...' Further down the river, there were problems: 'After a long contest with a violent adverse wind, and very turbulent water, pass under, on the south shore, Newark; a castellated house...' Nevertheless he was able to reach Greenock in time for dinner, and to return to Glasgow that night.[5]

Pennant, in the manner of his time, took the problems philosophically. Later on, people looking back from the steamboat era thought differently.

The minister of Dunoon, in a footnote to his article about the parish in the *New Statistical Account* (1843),[6] recorded:

> A gentleman resident in Glasgow has also mentioned, that, about thirty-two years ago [i.e. 1811] desiring to convey his family for summer residence to the village of Gourock … they set out from Glasgow in the morning in one of the passage-boats at that time plying on the river, and denominated, not very appropriately, 'Flies.' The whole of that day they were occupied in making good their way the length of Bowling Bay, not nearly half-way from Glasgow to Greenock, and there came to anchor for the night. Weighing next morning and proceeding to *sea*, the wind being contrary, after spending the whole day in buffeting the waves of the Clyde, they were forced to put back, returning the second night to Bowling Bay. The third day they made the next attempt and succeeded in making Port-Glasgow, in the afternoon, where he took post-horses, leaving the *fly* in disgust; and having seen his family housed in Gourock, he returned on the *fourth* day to Glasgow, weary, sick and exhausted…

Such were the problems of travel which Henry Bell foresaw, correctly, would be alleviated by travel in boats propelled by steam.

He had been considering the possibility for many years, but of just when and how it first came to his attention it is now impossible to be certain. According to Morris: 'It appears from Mr Bell's own writings that it was at Borrowstowness, in 1786, when with Messrs Shaw, that his mind was strongly impressed with the steam-boat system.'[7] That seems a suspiciously convenient date, for someone trying to claim precedence, being a couple of years before Symington's experiments of 1788–9. Yet in 1786 Miller was already carrying out his experiments into paddle-wheel propulsion at Leith, not far away. During the summer of 1787 the possibility of steam propulsion was considered by Miller, and was mentioned in his pamphlet published later that year.[8] Bell is likely to have been aware of Symington's 1788–9 experiments, the results of which were well publicised. Symington himself claimed that Bell had witnessed the trials of the second boat late in 1789;[9] he might have heard about Symington's work from Rennie, who had seen the engine under construction. It seems to have been about this time that Bell moved from London to Glasgow, and in any case the trials near Falkirk took place in his home territory. So it can probably be said safely that it was at this period that Bell first started to think about steam propulsion for boats.

Bell may, or may not, at some stage have approached James Watt for advice – opinions vary. If he did so, he evidently got the usual Watt brush-off.[10]

There can be no doubt that Bell was aware of, and probably familiar with, *Charlotte Dundas* in her successive forms. Few people with an interest in such matters and resident in Glasgow – as he was at the time – can have failed to be so. Bell too had another potential link with *Charlotte Dundas*: Alexander Hart, who built the hull of the first vessel of that name, was the son of George Hart of Shaw and Hart,[11] by whom he had been employed – and he appears to have kept in touch with his former employers, for he was to take *Comet* to them for overhaul in 1813. Nevertheless this seems to have been a subject on which he had little if anything to say.

Others were less reticent. There are suggestions that he made visits to Carron Ironworks while the machinery was being built, intruding himself among the workmen to the extent of making a nuisance of himself.[12] Symington himself states that Bell was a frequent visitor to *Charlotte Dundas* when laid up near Falkirk.[13]

It is suggested too that he visited *Charlotte Dundas* in company with Robert Fulton. This is much more problematic, as indeed is Bell's entire relationship with Fulton. As early as 1816, in an attempt to claim precedence over the Americans, he sent a letter to the editor of the *Caledonian Mercury*. In this extraordinary document he wrote that at the request of 'Mr Fulton, the American engineer' he had called on Miller at Dalswinton to find out how he had succeeded in his steam boat plan, that Miller gave him information, that he had sent drawings to Fulton, and that Fulton two years later wrote that he had constructed a steam boat from 'the different drawings of machinery I had sent'.[14] The snag to this is that if Bell sent details of the 1788–9 experiments to Fulton soon after they had been completed, it would have been too early in Fulton's career for them to have been of much value; but if he sent them at the time when Fulton was indeed commencing on the experimental work which would lead to success, then it would have been too late, for steam boat design had already moved on, and Fulton would presumably have found out all he needed to know of them direct from Symington.

On the principle that there is probably a germ of truth in this somewhere, it is conceivable that what Bell sent to Fulton was details of the second *Charlotte Dundas*. Although the layout of the *Clermont* owed nothing to that vessel, it is noteworthy that the layout of horizontal cylinder driving stern paddle wheel re-appears in the *New Orleans* of 1811, built by Fulton's associate Nicholas Roosevelt and the first steamer on the Mississippi.[15]

Bell, however, continued to enhance his story. In 1824 he claimed that Fulton had called on him in 1803, and again in 1804 – which from Fulton's known activities during those years is improbable – that he, Bell, had written to the American government on the utility of steam navigation on their rivers, and that they had appointed Fulton to correspond with him.[16] By 1825 or thereabouts he had embroidered the tale even more. He told Telford's protégé Joseph Mitchell that he had accompanied Fulton on a visit to the vessel constructed by Symington (presumably the *Charlotte Dundas*) – and that Fulton subsequently wrote for Bell to join him in New York, where he took the leading part in constructing Fulton's boat, and after seeing it at work on the Hudson returned to Glasgow.[17]

The *Clermont* was built during the spring of 1807, and her trial trips took place in August. It would not have been easy for Bell to combine building the *Clermont* in New York with building the Baths Inn in Helensburgh, and galvanising that burgh's quiescent civic powers into life – particularly considering that a transatlantic voyage in those days was a matter of weeks. It seems that, to Bell's tendency toward creative reinterpretation of historical evidence, there must sadly be added a great capacity for self-delusion. All the more to be regretted in one whose real achievements were great enough to stand on their own merits.

Speculation on the hidden truths within Bell's statements could fill an entire paper – but not very profitably. It does seem probable that he and Fulton were in contact, and biographers of Fulton have accepted this, although the sources seem to be on the Bell side.[18] According to Brian Osborne, no correspondence between Bell and Fulton can be traced in the American archives which hold Fulton's papers.[19]

Likewise, tales of early experiments made by Bell with models and pleasure boats[20] must be treated with circumspection. But from about 1807 he was discussing the possibility of propelling a boat by machinery with John Robertson,[21] who provided the engine to pump water at the Baths Inn. Robertson too had seen the *Charlotte Dundas* lying in the Forth & Clyde Canal. It seems clear that Bell's programme of trials and experiments which would lead to the *Comet* started in 1809, for that is what he wrote in his pamphlet *Observations on the Utility of Applying Steam Engines to Vessels, &c* which was published four years later, at which date he had little inducement to exaggerate. In this he wrote that in 1809 he attempted to make a small model which was successful enough to convince him that an engine could be made to drive a vessel in all weathers; and that in 1810 he built a small boat, 13 feet long by 5 feet beam in which he tried a great many experiments, erecting different machines, so that by 1811 he was fully convinced that a vessel of any size could be worked by steam.[22]

Unfortunately Bell had made the error of failing to give credit where due. In this case that meant to John Thomson, another former millwright who had become a skilled and experienced maker and erector of steam engines. Thomson had come to know Bell during 1811 while staying at the Baths Inn for the benefit of the sea air. Not long after Bell's pamphlet was published Thomson produced his own, in counterblast.[23] While at the Baths Inn, he said, he had had many conversations with Bell about the uses of steam engines and the working of vessels by steam – knowing that they were used to a great extent on the rivers of the United States. (So by this date, even if not before, it can be taken that Bell was aware of the work of Fulton.)

According to Thomson, after he returned from Helensburgh Bell called on him and said he had a boat being built at Greenock, which he proposed to use for experiments to ascertain if it was possible to work a passage boat by hand from Glasgow to Helensburgh, and into which he wished Thomson to put the machinery. The boat was the same as that described by Bell in his *Observations...* It was built with an opening in the stern, *Charlotte Dundas*-style, into which were fitted paddles mounted on a shaft driven through bevel gears by a handle within the boat. When at Bell's request this vessel was tried out on the Paisley Canal, so much water was thrown into the boat that it sank before the two men on board could reach the bank.

The opening was closed in, and successive experiments were made on the Clyde with paddles in various positions on the boat, including the sides, but always with limited success. Bell seems to have attempted to maintain the fiction that he was thinking in terms of manual power, for he told Thomson that it was of no use to him if a stout boy, by application of mechanical powers, could not row a boat with ten or twelve people on board – to which Thomson retorted that he knew this to be impossible, for a man could apply his whole strength to an oar as well as to any other machine. Despite this, and after many evasions by Bell, Thomson and he started to discuss financial arrangements for, and the technicalities of, a steam boat for the Clyde, to the extent that Thomson prepared sketches of the parts, followed by a complete drawing of boat and machinery. Bell borrowed this, and in due course returned it. Shortly after that he called on Thomson and settled up for the experimental work Thomson had done, to the extent of £23. The implication in Thomson's pamphlet is that Bell had used the plans to obtain machinery elsewhere, for a boat he had already ordered. But Thomson retained the paddle boat, and continued to experiment on his own account.[24]

Clearly Bell was, to say the least, economical with the truth in his dealings with Thomson. He may, perhaps, have detected a potentially dangerous rival. If so, his concern would prove to be well-justified, although his method of tackling the problem had probably aggravated it. At any rate he was by this stage well on the way to having a steamboat built without any further involvement by Thomson.

To build a steamboat in 1811 meant bringing together three separate disciplines: those of the engineer, to build the engine and machinery, of the boilermaker, and of the shipbuilder. Of these three, the first two were already associated with one another, the third not at all with either. But practitioners of all these disciplines, fortunately, were well-established around Glasgow and the Firth of Clyde.

The engine for Bell's steamboat was already in existence. John Robertson had gone into business on his own account the previous year, with works off North Hanover Street, Glasgow. He had already achieved a good reputation as a builder of small steam engines, and in 1811 he built one as a speculation. It was (and is, for it still exists) a 'portable' engine – that is to say it was self-contained, and capable of being moved complete from one location to another, rather than being built into the structure of an engine house. In appearance and layout it seems to owe much to Matthew Murray's portable engine of 1805, which was mentioned at the end of chapter one. As in Murray's engine, a vertical cylinder is mounted above a framework made from iron castings. This frame also incorporates a tank containing the condenser, and the air-pump which extracts air and condensate from it. Gone, however, is the awkwardly inaccessible beam mounted below the framework: instead, connecting rods link the crosshead down to a pair of end-pivotted levers working up and down beside it. Downward extensions of these levers are connected by a rod passing beneath the framework. Mounted centrally on this, beneath the cylinder, is a connecting rod driving upwards onto a crank on the end of the crankshaft – the main part of this is located to one side of the main structure. The cylinder, on the engine as built, had a diameter of 11½ inches and a stroke of 16 inches, and steam was distributed by a short slide valve of Murray's type, driven by an eccentric on the crankshaft – a slip eccentric which enabled the engine to be reversed. Also mounted on the crankshaft were a large flywheel and a pinion which formed the first part of the drive to the paddles.[25]

The layout is neat and well-thought out – primitive by later standards, but not primaeval (unlike the engine of *Charlotte Dundas*, which was advanced in concept but less so in construction). Robertson's engine was not only more accessible than Murray's portable engine, but also more compact, and very much more so than the usual beam engine of the period: an engine intended for land use, to drive machinery in a mill or factory, but eminently suitable, by the standards of the time, for mounting in a boat. The chance to purchase this engine must have been for Bell an opportunity not to be missed, although his decision to do so did not help relations with Thomson, who had reasonably expected to build the machinery himself for their projected steamboat. At any rate in April 1812 Bell agreed with Robertson to buy the engine for £165, and Robertson was to provide boiler mountings for a further £27. A guinea changed hands to confirm the bargain.[26]

For a boiler Bell went to John Napier's Foundry, which had a good reputation for ironfounding, and smith-work. Bell had had many previous dealings with John Napier, and from time to time had discussed his ideas for steam navigation with him. By this date however John Napier was growing old and manufacture of the boiler was supervised by his son David Napier (1790–1869). David Napier must have had engineering in the blood – from early childhood he recalled, in his father's works which were then at Dumbarton, an atmospheric rotative engine ponderously at work night and day. It drove the machinery which bored the barrels of cannon needed for the war with the French. In 1802 the works were moved to Howard Street, Glasgow, and Napier seems to have had the run of the place – never serving a regular apprenticeship to anything, he wrote, but putting his hand to everything. At the age of twelve he not only saw the *Charlotte Dundas* when she came to Port Dundas in 1803 but went on board, where he carefully observed the layout of the boiler and machinery. He later referred to Symington as 'a gentleman I have had the pleasure of meeting.' By the age of twenty he was in charge of his father's works; in 1813 John Napier died.[27]

Very little is known for certain of the boiler for Bell's steamboat. Napier recollected, however:

> that we had considerable difficulty with the boiler; not having been accustomed to make boilers with internal flues, we made them first of cast iron, but finding that would not do, we tried our hand with malleable iron, and ultimately succeeded, with the aid of a liberal supply of horse dung, in getting the boiler filled.[28]

Unusually for this early period, therefore, the boiler had an internal flue (or perhaps flues). In this, presumably, were grate and fire – which may be construed not only as an aid to efficiency, but also as a safety precaution to keep burning coals and hot ashes well away from a wooden hull. Several sources suggest that the boiler was externally fired, but the above seems more likely. Horse dung, and also oatmeal, inserted into a boiler were specifics for sealing leaking seams. It is likely that the boiler was otherwise of the waggon type, and that the steam pressure was around 7 lbs per sq. inch.[29]

Engines and boilers were still new technology in 1811, but shipbuilders had the accumulated knowledge of centuries upon which to draw. For the hull of his vessel, Henry Bell went to a shipbuilder of experience and good reputation – John Wood senior. He had been in business since the 1780s, first in Port Glasgow, then in Greenock, then from 1810 back in Port Glasgow. Wood contracted to build the ship, and work started in October 1811. Then Wood died the following month. The yard was taken over by his son, also John Wood (1788–1860), who had been managing it; he was joined by his younger brother Charles.[30] They continued the contract. So the *Comet* had the benefit of being, in all its three departments, the product of young men early in their careers, who were all keen and competent. In each case, too, she would prove to be the first in a long line of steamships with which they would be concerned.

Bell's steamboat was built of wood, as were all ships at that period. According to her owner, she was 40 feet long, 10½ feet beam with projections of 1 foot 10 inches on either side over the paddles, and a hold 8 feet deep.[31] But many other figures approximating to these have been given: consulting half a dozen different sources produces half a dozen different sets of figures. Her tonnage, ie capacity, was about 25. She had a bluff bow, but her hull narrowed gradually towards the stern, in the manner of sailing ships of the time. By May or June 1812 she was far enough advanced for engine and boiler to be installed. John Robertson had them loaded into a gabbart – a sailing barge of the type then in general use about the Clyde – and took them down to Port Glasgow.[32]

Boiler and engine were installed alongside one another, with (probably) the boiler to port and the engine to starboard. Napier had also supplied some castings, said to have been for the engine[33] but as this had long since been completed they seem more likely to have been for the spur gears and associated equipment which constituted the drive to the paddles – such could have been described loosely as 'for the engine'. On either side of the boat were two sets of paddles. Each comprised four paddles mounted radially around a shaft and so at 90 degrees to each other. (To refer to these simple constructions as paddle wheels seems scarcely justified.) Robertson had wanted one set on each side, considering that the aft set would do little work in the broken water astern of the forward set, but Bell had insisted on two sets. Drawings show the forward paddles positioned at 45 degrees to the aft ones,[34] so that two of the forward paddles were just entering and leaving the water when one of the aft ones was submerged to its deepest – which looks like an attempt to even out the thrust from successive paddles. A tall sheet-iron funnel on the centre line of the boat was evidently cranked at its foot to line up with the offset boiler – a feature which was exaggerated in some early engravings of the vessel. The funnel doubled as a mast, for the vessel was rigged for sailing with a square sail and a jib – and indeed eventually had a reputation for sailing well.[35] Over the ensuing decades, steamships would normally be rigged to go by sail as well as by steam, and it seems to have been late in the nineteenth century before ships were regularly equipped to go by steam alone. Clyde steamers were still carrying sails during the first decade of the twentieth century.[36]

Passenger accommodation, according to Bell, comprised a cockpit at the stern, with stairs leading to a cabin 10 feet 4 inches long by 7 feet 6 inches 'elegantly furnished with sofas all round, &c'. Ahead of this came the boiler and engine, open to the sky, and ahead of that another cabin, 12 feet 6 inches by 10 feet 6 inches, described as 'steerage', with seating all round. The deck had seats around it, and each of the paddle boxes incorporated a water closet. For night-time use the stern cabin could be divided into three by partitions – two of the resulting 'apartments' each contained 'two handsome beds' – and there were four beds available in steerage also.[37] This provision of night-time accommodation is a surprise, considering that Glasgow to Greenock or Helensburgh was scarcely an overnight voyage. Maybe it was intended for use by the crew, or maybe passengers were to be allowed on board over night before an early start, in the manner of later Hebridean ferries. Or perhaps Bell's ambitions were already looking much further afield.

Robertson later recalled 'a very neat craft', prettily painted of different colours, and with a figurehead of a lady with red cheeks and a coloured dress.[38]

In March 1812 Bell engaged William M'Kenzie to be master of his steamboat, and sent him to Wood's yard to superintend her building.[39] Then, as completion of the vessel approached, a problem arose: Bell had run out of funds to pay Wood – even though, apparently, the purpose of the sale of the Baths Inn had been to finance the steamboat. Eventually he found a guarantor for the sum involved – probably Mr Kibble of Dalmonach Print Works, which Bell was at this time rebuilding,[40] and this was sufficient for Wood to release the vessel, which had been lying completed in his yard.

The time when Bell was planning his steamboat and having her built was also the time of the celestial phenomenon known as Great Comet of 1811. Great comets are exceptionally bright, and rare. This one was noticed for the first time by astronomers on 25 March 1811, and for the last time on 12 August 1812, having in the meantime reached its brightest in the late autumn of 1811. It was visible to the naked eye for some 260 days, a record which remained unbroken until 1997. It has been calculated that this comet passes the earth every 3,000 years or so, which is why it is now unfamiliar. In 1811 it was a sensation, and it attracted immense public interest among what had become a nation of fascinated comet-watchers.[41]

Comets are traditionally supposed to portend dire events. This one seems to have been particularly noticeable from the steamboat *New Orleans* as she made her pioneering way down the Ohio and Mississippi rivers that autumn – and its appearance was promptly followed by earthquakes and unprecedented floods. It was later considered to have foretold Napoleon's disastrous invasion of Russia in 1812. Comets are also considered to have a beneficial effect on wine vintages, and it is remarkable that after a series of bad vintages during the early years of the nineteenth century, that of 1811 produced some of the best wines ever. As recently as 1992 the feature film *The Year of the Comet* had as its theme the discovery of a bottle of 1811 wine, and the heroine's attempts against all opposition to recover it. Then, fact perhaps exceeding fiction, when a bottle of 1811 'comet vintage' Château d'Yquem was sold in 2011, it reached a world record price, for a white wine, of £75,000.

Such have been the effects, then and now, of the phenomenon after which Bell decided to name his steamboat. The name *Comet* was painted on her paddleboxes, and she was launched with steam up on 24 July, 1812.[42]

FIVE

The Comet at Work –
and Her Competitors

The maiden voyage of the *Comet* took place, doubtless after earlier trials, on Thursday 6 August 1812. With Henry Bell and John Robertson on board, she went from Port Glasgow to the Broomielaw, Glasgow, in three and a half hours.[1]

By then, Bell had already issued a circular, which was published in the press, to the effect that he had 'at much expense, fitted up a handsome vessel to ply upon the River Clyde, between Glasgow and Greenock, to sail by the power of wind, air, and steam' and that he intended that 'the vessel shall leave the Broomielaw on Tuesdays, Thursdays, and Saturdays, about midday, or at such hour thereafter as may answer from the state of the tide; and to leave Greenock on Mondays, Wednesdays and Fridays, in the morning, to suit the tide…' The fare was to be four shillings in the best cabin, three shillings in 'the second'. He continued, the circular went on, his establishment at Helensburgh Baths, and a small vessel would be in readiness to convey passengers off the *Comet* from Greenock to Helensburgh. At that date there was no pier at Helensburgh at which the *Comet* could have come alongside. Details of the *Comet*'s hours of sailing could be obtained from agents at the Broomielaw and at Greenock.[2]

'By the power of wind, air and steam': *Comet*'s engine was known to be of low power in relation to the size of the boat. It may be, too, that in putting first the wind, the old familiar form of propulsion, Bell was seeking to reassure potential passengers that they would not be wholly at the mercy of the new form of propulsion, steam. It is also clear that Bell intended, as was usual, to turn the tide to advantage, or at least minimise its disadvantages.

The 'power of wind' and 'air' looks at first sight like duplication. Possibly with 'air' Bell was referring to air pressure, the pressure of the atmosphere, which with a steam engine working at low steam pressure would still be making a greater contribution towards the onward progress of the boat than the pressure of steam itself. But detailed research into the usage of the time would be needed to state this as a certainty.

At any rate, if intentions became fact it is likely that *Comet*'s first voyage carrying passengers was on Saturday 8 August, and after that she seems to have gone into regular service. On her way up and down the Clyde she called at all the ferries. Her downstream terminal was at Greenock, except on Saturdays when she went over to Helensburgh for the weekend, and presumably anchored off-shore. In addition to the captain, William McKenzie, the crew of about seven men included Robert Robertson, who was John Robertson's brother, as engineer and Duncan McInnes, a Highlander, as pilot. On at least some occasions there was a piper too. The usual journey time was about five hours.[3] That was if all went well: one of the reasons for regulating departure times to match the tides was to ensure sufficient depth of water for a boat of 4-foot draught over the shoals – although the work of improvement to the Clyde had already achieved much, it still had much more to achieve. Sometimes the *Comet* did go aground. On one such occasion Margaret Bell was on board. 'What was done then?' asked an enquirer, years afterwards: 'Oh,' came the reply, 'the men just stepped over the side and pushed her off the shoal.'[4]

Any piece of equipment or machinery which represents a revolutionary advance in technology is certain to be subject to successive modifications, in the light of experience, over the period it is in use. That *Comet* was fully subject to this process is clear. What is not so clear is exactly what was done, and when. Accounts are sometimes vague, sometimes contradictory. The pros and cons have been considered in detail elsewhere,[5] and will not be comprehensively re-examined here, although what is written here on the subject is believed to be accurate.

There is no doubt that after a couple of months or so substantial modifications were seen to be needed. The boat was too slow, with a maximum speed no more than 5 mph, to compete with coaches on land and was not being well supported by the public. Bell consulted engineers well known in Glasgow – including Robertson Buchanan, whose treatise on steamboats would appear within a few years, and a Mr Baird who was presumably a member of the noted canal-engineering family of that name. Bell then arranged with Robertson that he would fit a larger cylinder, of 12½-inch diameter by 16-inch stroke, to the engine. This increased the total price of the engine to £365, including the original sum, which was still unpaid. But it also increased the power of the engine to 4 hp and the speed of the boat to 7 mph or so. That was an improvement, although the boat remained unable to make headway against the strongest headwinds and tides. It had been observed that the aft set of paddles did little work and made the boat difficult to steer: one set of paddles was removed and, it seems, the other replaced by a pair of paddle wheels, each of which had six or more floats.[6]

Like this the *Comet* continued to operate through the autumn and into the winter – on one December voyage downstream she had to break her way cautiously through the ice, and then, perhaps because slow progress meant she had not kept up with the ebbing tide, went aground near Govan, and again near Bowling.[7] But she was warmer than a coach on land, and usually as quick, and cheaper.[8] The steamboat was becoming established – but Bell was not making any money.

Even so, although meeting the demand for travel between Glasgow and Helensburgh may originally have prompted Bell to have the *Comet* built, before very long his visionary imagination was soaring far and wide. As a preliminary, presumably, to taking her further afield, on 13 May 1813 Bell had her registered at Port Glasgow, her first registration as she had previously 'been employed in inland navigation'. The name of her master is given as James Bruce – Mackenzie, unwell, had left the previous December. The registration certificate notes that *Comet* had an 'iron funnel mast' and was 'furnished with a steam engine and its machinery by which she sails'. Her length, 'from the Fore-part of the Main Stem to the After-part of the Stern Post aloft', was given as 43 feet 6 inches.[9]

By then another, larger, steamboat had been in service between Glasgow and Greenock since March. Either in reaction to this, or just to spread the steamboat gospel, or more probably a bit of both, Bell took *Comet* through the Forth & Clyde Canal to the Firth of Forth. She visited his old employers, Shaw & Hart, at Bo'ness, where some refitting work was done – but probably not very much, for by 24 May she was in Leith Harbour. She had carried some passengers from Bo'ness, and she seems to have run short trips from Leith[10] – a 'jaunting boat' was Bell's later description of her at this stage.[11] At the time he had evidently had much more ambitious plans, but, as the *Edinburgh Evening Courant* later reported, 'The Comet steam-boat, after getting into the Firth of Forth, found her machinery of so little power in the rough water of the ocean, that the idea of proceeding to London was necessarily abandoned.'[12] By the beginning of June, *Comet* was back on the Clyde, having in the process taken a becalmed sailing vessel in tow and brought her to Greenock.[13] She went back into service on her original route. Her hull may, at some time in this period, have been lengthened,[14] although not to any great extent, presumably, for she was still under-powered.

In all this, Bell had spent far more than he could afford, and in 1813 some of his expenses were defrayed by a group of prominent fellow-citizens of the region. These included, perhaps surprisingly, Kirkman Finlay, who had become MP for Glasgow.[15]

Thomson and the *Elizabeth*

The larger steamboat which had been in service between Glasgow and Greenock since March was the *Elizabeth*, which was the second steamboat on the Clyde and had been running daily since 9 March 1813. The moving spirit behind this vessel was none other than John Thomson who, spurned by Henry Bell, had had her laid down, by John Wood at Port Glasgow as early as March 1812. A hiatus followed, caused by what Thomson referred to as 'certain private circumstances' and which may perhaps be construed as 'difficulty in raising the money', and work recommenced the following October, leading to her launch on 20 November.[16] *Elizabeth* was a substantially bigger boat than *Comet* at 58 feet 9 inches over stem and stern post, and more powerful, with an engine of 9 hp or thereabouts.[17]

There is uncertainty as to both her ownership and the builder of her engine: Thomson in his own account is reticent on these points. She is often regarded as Thomson's, where any indication of ownership is given at all, but important early sources state that she belonged to 'Mr Hutchinson, a brewer of Glasgow'.[18] Maybe Hutchinson had come to Thomson's rescue, financially. As to the engine, opinion, both early and recent, seems to be equally divided as to whether, as might be expected, Thomson's own firm built it,[19] or whether it was built by James Cook, a respected Glasgow engineer.[20] Both may be true – perhaps Thomson sub-contracted all or part of the work to Cook, or perhaps the *Elizabeth* was re-engined at some stage. Such uncertainties bedevil the entire history of early steamboats.

Elizabeth's accommodation was clearly intended to outdo that of *Comet* in sumptuousness: the best cabin was 21 feet long, carpeted and seated all round, a sofa at one end with a mirror above, bookshelves 'containing a collection of the best authors', and 'twelve small windows, each furnished with marone [i.e. maroon] curtains, with tassels, fringes and velvet cornices, ornamented with gilt ornaments, having altogether a very rich effect.[21] This was the Regency period, noted for such decorative style; in the manner of their accommodation, too, these early steamboats seem to have had a precursor in that of the canal passage boats.

Despite this luxury, fares by the *Elizabeth* were cheaper than *Comet* – four shillings in the best cabin – and the duration of the voyage between Glasgow and Greenock was less, at under four hours. When wind and tide were favourable, she sometimes did it in 2 hours and 45 minutes.[22]

Initially, as might be expected, *Elizabeth* was very successful, on occasion carrying more than 100 passengers at a time. But within two years she in turn had been outclassed, and in 1814 she sailed south to bring the benefits of steam navigation to the River Mersey.[23]

Robertson and the *Clyde*

In the spring of 1813, that lay in the future. That Thomson should have set up in competition with Bell so promptly is perhaps no surprise: and that Wood should build a steamboat for him without apparent hesitation is probably explained by the maxim that business is business. But what does raise eyebrows is to find that the third steamboat to be placed on the Clyde was not only once again the work of John Wood, but was instigated by John Robertson. To be charitable, one can only suppose that it was becoming clear that, while there was going to be traffic for three or more steamboats, Bell's resources were too much overstretched for him to meet the demand, and Robertson felt he deserved some of the benefit.

This vessel, the *Clyde*, was launched on 6 February 1814, and appears to have gone into service between Glasgow and Greenock a few weeks after the *Elizabeth*, with one boat leaving Glasgow and the other Greenock each morning, and vice versa in the afternoon. At 72 feet over stem and sternpost she was larger again than *Elizabeth*, but with her Clyde steamboats had reached the sort of length that would become usual over the ensuing years. Her accommodation included for the first time a space for goods – this was some 15 feet long, between the after cabin and the engine. Henry Bell himself enthused about this feature, pointing out that it would be very advantageous to the public, as *Clyde* would be a much more regular trader than any vessel that must wait for a fair wind. The engine itself was of 12 or 14 hp, built by Robertson; John Robertson and Robert Steven were joint owners of the vessel. Among her crew was William Mackenzie, evidently now recovered, as pilot – he was promoted to master early in 1815. Her route sometimes extended to Gourock.[24]

With three steamboats in regular service during the summer of 1813 between Glasgow and Greenock, it soon became clear for all to see that they were causing a dramatic decline in road traffic between those places: turnpike trust income was substantially reduced, some stage coaches were withdrawn, and the Post Office became concerned at the reduction in traffic by Mail Coach.[25] More and more people were taking an interest in steamboats.

The *Glasgow*

A particularly interested observer of this process was Henry Creighton, who was Boulton, Watt & Co.'s local engineering representative.[26] 'Verily, verily, there hath been little done but steamboat scheming these last 2 months,' he wrote on 21 July 1813 to his brother William in Birmingham. Although he did not entirely approve of the bright, even gaudy, appearance of steamboats ('…is not the steamboat to be a marvellous pretty thing, gilt like a heathen god and shining like a peacock's tail…') he nevertheless considered that for one 'who is inclined to speculate on steamboat property there is no time like the present.' Shares were sold for £100 or £200 each. There was a steamboat on the stocks to be called *Glasgow*, a scheme for another to be called *Greenock*, and a third was planned, possibly to be called *Hercules*, to haul lighters up and down the river.[27]

The *Glasgow*, then, was owned not by an individual or a couple of partners, but by a consortium of investors. Such would become the usual arrangement. Henry Bell may or may not have invested in the *Glasgow*, but he certainly superintended the construction of this ship by John Wood & Co. He also supplied the engine, which was built by Anderson & Campbell of Greenock, and the vessel was launched that September. All this should have cemented Bell's position as leader of the steamboat movement: regrettably, it was to do nothing of the sort. For although *Glasgow*'s hull, 69 feet from stem to stern and 15 feet 2 inches beam, proved eventually to be very successful, the engine was a failure. It had to be replaced. Bell found himself involved in litigation, which cannot have helped his ever-precarious financial position.[28]

A new engine was supplied in 1814 by James Cook. Cook was described by David Napier as 'the oldest and most respectable engine maker in Glasgow';[29] he had been in business since about 1785 as a millwright and engineer. His main product was machinery for sugar mills: these initially had been powered by water wheels and windmills, and latterly by steam engines.[30] That he was indeed a man of talent was confirmed by the design of the engine he provided for *Glasgow*, and also for the *Argyle*, which was being built about this time and will be mentioned shortly. These were side-lever engines:[31] that is to say the end-pivotted, up-and-down levers of Robertson's engine for the *Comet* were replaced by rocking levers, or beams, pivotted centrally. Positioned low down on either side of the engine, at one end they were driven by connecting rods down from the piston-rod crosshead, and at the other they drove upwards by a connecting rod to the crankshaft. This layout, simple, accessible, compact and with a low centre of gravity, was to become the conventional one for marine steam engines for decades to come – so much so that in the 1840s and 1850s a representation of a side-lever engine appeared on the uniform coat buttons worn by engineers in the Royal Navy.[32] The engines for *Glasgow* and *Argyle* appear to have been the first examples of side-lever engines – unless, of course, Cook had earlier supplied one for the *Elizabeth*. Either way the credit for their introduction is evidently due to James Cook.

In parenthesis, however, it must be noted that when Robert Fulton had taken out his second US patent, which was granted in 1811, he had included among much else a form of side-lever layout – more complex, though, than the form brought into use by Cook, as drive from the levers to the crankshaft was indirect. We cannot be sure whether Cook was aware of this patent or not: it seems more likely to have been a case of two good minds working independently on the same problem and hitting on the same solution. Boulton, Watt & Co. on the other hand did become aware of it, for a copy of the patent survived among Boulton & Watt mss[33] – but there again one cannot be sure when they became so, possibly not until J. C. Dyer had been in touch with them in 1814.

At any rate *Glasgow*, with her new engine (cylinder diameter 22 inches, piston stroke 2 feet, working at 45 strokes per minute),[34] became the fastest steamboat on the river and was known to reach Greenock, with the tide, in 2 hours and 10 minutes.[35] Her route was extended to Largs. Sir John Rennie (son of the earlier John Rennie), in his presidential address to the Institution of Civil Engineers in 1846, expressed the opinion that while earlier steamboats had been very imperfect, *Glasgow* with Cook's engine was more perfect and powerful than any previous, and served as a model for others.[36]

During 1814 at least six more steamboats went into service on the Clyde – the products of all that scheming the previous year, no doubt. The same year saw steamboats go into service on the Firth of Forth, and the Firth of Tay – they will be described in chapter six. They also went into service on many other rivers and estuaries around the coast of Britain in 1813 (a few) and 1814 (many more). These will be described in chapter eight.

The Clyde Steamboats of 1814

Launched onto the Clyde in 1814 were the steamboats *Trusty* (in February), *Princess Charlotte* (March), *Industry* (May), *Prince of Orange*, *Margery* and *Argyle* (all in June).[37] The sudden irruption of steamboats onto the river was greatly aided by the presence in Glasgow of engineering firms which, since expiry of Watt's patent, had been turning increasingly to manufacture of stationary steam engines and boilers. Now they were able to add marine engines and boilers to their range. Napier and Robertson have already been mentioned; Cook was also one of this group, and other important manufacturers who were to do so in 1814 or soon after were George Dobbie, Duncan McArthur & Co., and the Greenhead Foundry Company.[38] Of the steamboats launched in 1814, *Trusty* and *Industry* were engined by Dobbie, and *Margery* and *Argyle* by Cook. *Princess Charlotte* and *Prince of Orange*, on the other hand, marked the entry of Boulton, Watt & Co. into the home market for steamboat machinery.[39]

This series of boats also marked increases in the numbers of shipbuilders building steamboat hulls and in the locations at which they were built. *Trusty* and *Margery* were built at Dumbarton by Archibald MacLachlan, the first steamboats of several that he would build over the next few years; *Princess Charlotte* and *Prince of Orange* were built at Greenock by the old-established firm of James Munn; *Industry* was built at Fairlie by William Fyfe, the only steamer ever built by a firm which would later become famous as yacht-builders, and *Argyle* was built at Port Glasgow by Alex. Martin & Co.[40]

Henry Creighton, when he wrote to his brother in July 1813, had mentioned a proposed steamboat to be called, perhaps, *Hercules*, which would carry parcels and such passengers as did not mind a slow journey, and would tow a lighter of 30 or 40 tons. There were to be three lighters, two always unloading or loading at Glasgow and Greenock, and the third 'on the road'.[41] This promising scheme does not seem to have come to fruition in that form, but it may well have been the germ of an idea which led to construction of the steamboats *Trusty* and *Industry*. Both were used primarily as 'luggage boats' carrying goods and parcels, and were also used to tow lighters. They were ordered by a Mr D. Cochrane, described variously as merchant or tanner, who was acting apparently on behalf of a syndicate based in Beith, Ayrshire. Beith is well inland, but may help to explain the choice of a builder located at Fairlie, the nearest point on the coast, for the boat which became *Industry* – particularly since Fyfe was a native of Kilbirnie, not far from Beith, and indeed built her of oak grown in his home parish. Dobbie provided *Industry* with a 10 hp side-lever engine – *Trusty*'s engine, of the same power, was presumably similar.[42]

Trusty, regrettably, was wrecked,[43] but *Industry* survived for longer than any of her contemporaries – Fyfe must have built well. In 1828 her engine was replaced by another side-lever engine, of 14 nominal hp, built by Caird & Co. of Greenock. With this she soldiered on down the years, retaining drive by spur gears from crankshaft to paddle wheel shaft when such things had long been out-dated on newer vessels. With cogs constantly giving way, the gear wheels needed constant replacement, and the grinding noise they made when working gained for *Industry* the nickname 'the coffee mill'. Eventually in 1862 she was in a collision and badly damaged. She was laid up in Bowling Harbour and there the hull of what was by then the oldest surviving steamship gradually deteriorated until by the 1880s it was beyond preserving. Her 1828 engine, however, was removed and went to Glasgow's Kelvingrove Museum.[44]

A lot of original thought clearly went into design and layout of *Prince of Orange*, which is described in detail by Robertson Buchanan in his *Elementary Treatise... Princess Charlotte* was probably similar. To cope with the shoals and shallows of the Clyde, *Prince of Orange* was designed to draw no more than 3 feet 6 inches when fully laden, and to this end was made flat-bottomed. The rectangular boiler extended from one side of the hull to the other and for the first time a pair of steam engines was installed. These were each of 4 hp and their cylinders, vertical as usual, were recessed into the forward corners of the boiler, presumably to conserve heat. The connecting rod of each drove an overhead beam: this was not, however, a centrally pivoted rocking beam, but worked up-and-down, pivoted at its forward end on a support mounted on deck. From an intermediate point on the beam a downward connecting rod drove a crank on the end of a shaft: this extended across the boat to a crank driven by the other engine, and also carried spur gears to drive the paddle-wheel shafts. No flywheel was needed, and the whole arrangement was better balanced, both mechanically and for the trim of the boat, than the then-usual arrangement of engine alongside offset boiler, in which any substantial change in the water level caused the vessel to list. The engine room was roofed over, and supplied with air for the furnaces through a channel within the boat from an intake mounted on the foredeck. The cowl of this could be turned to the wind – it must have been one of the earliest examples of equipment of this type. The cabin was heated by hot air – air from the proximity of the funnel was forced into it by a pump.

The length of the boat was 64 feet on the keel, the beam 12 feet. Her paddle wheels were 9 feet in diameter, and 2 feet 11 inches wide. An ingenious mechanism enabled the distance of the paddles from the wheel centres to be adjusted according to how deep the boat was in the water. Her hull was built of fir. The accommodation included fore-cabin, steward's room, ladies' cabin and principal cabin. The total cost of the boat was £2,300.

On the face of it, at 8 hp this vessel appears underpowered, yet her performance was considered satisfactory. Her shallow draft enabled her to ascend the White Cart Water to Paisley, the first steamboat to do so, on 25 July 1815. A vast crowd gathered to see her, and she left the following morning with passengers for Greenock and Gourock. In November 1816 *Prince of Orange* was recorded as plying on the Clyde, and again in 1817, although in 1816 sister ship *Princess Charlotte* was laid up.[45] Of their further career, reliable information seems lacking. Maybe they were re-named, or maybe they just did not last long – it is possible to cram too much technical innovation into a small space, however promising the result at first appears.

The *Margery* was built to the order of two Glasgow merchants, William Anderson and John McCubbin, and in due course named after Anderson's eldest daughter. She was laid down in 1813 at the Woodyard, Dumbarton, the yard of Archibald MacLachlan & Co. where *Trusty* was also built that winter. The yard would subsequently become closely associated with the name of Denny, and William Denny, who would later acquire the business, may well have worked on both of them as carpenter. *Margery*, with a keel length of 56 feet, was a small vessel. James Cook provided a side-lever engine of similar dimensions to the one he provided for *Glasgow*; it was supplied with steam at about 2 lb per sq. in. pressure by a flat-sided boiler with one or more flues. After her launch in June 1814 *Margery* went into service on the Clyde.[46]

Argyle, too, had a Cook side-lever engine and used steam at 2 lb per sq. in. pressure from a flued boiler alongside. The drive shaft to the paddle wheels appears to have passed through this. Her accommodation followed the pattern, apparently usual for the period, of fore-cabin, steward's room, ladies' cabin and main cabin; the latter was heated by a steam pipe beneath the seats. Again in the manner of the time, it was furnished elegantly, with hangings of scarlet cloth, sofas, Grecian-style chairs, looking glasses, Brussels carpet and a sixty-volume library. Her overall length was about

90 feet (72 feet on the keel), her beam, over the hull, 14 feet 6 inches but appearing much more, since the hull was surrounded by a gallery at deck-level approximating to the width of the sponsons which interrupted it. *Argyle* was the largest steamboat launched on to the Clyde so far, and one of the fastest, a 'capital seaworthy vessel' strongly built of oak and fir: her proprietors found her a good investment.[47]

Steamboats go south

Nevertheless, neither *Margery* nor *Argyle* stayed long on the Clyde. Henry Bell may have had a hand in the sale of either ship, or both.[48] Or he may not. At any rate, *Margery* was the first to leave. In November 1814 she was bought by a London company, Anthony Cortis & Co., for service on the Thames estuary. She went thither via the Forth & Clyde Canal and the east coast. To reduce her beam sufficiently to pass through the locks on the canal, her paddle wheels and sponsons had to be removed: so she was doubtless tracked through the canal by a horse. For this part of her voyage, a large party of Mr Anderson's friends and relations went along for the ride, at the invitation of Captain Cortis. The *Margery* then continued down the east coast under sail alone, it seems, reaching the Thames early in January.[49] Her subsequent varied career will be described in chapter eight.

Argyle was purchased in April 1815 by George Dodd, acting on behalf of R. Cheesewright & Co., a syndicate of nine members of which he was one. This had been set up to establish a steamboat service between London and Margate, already a popular resort. Dodd was a civil engineer – much of the preliminary work on London's Waterloo Bridge was his – with mechanical inclinations. His patented gun lock, proof against accidental discharge, had been approved by the Ordnance Board. Early in his career he had served in the Navy.[50] It was not him but a near-namesake, however, George Dodds, who would be responsible for bringing the steam railway locomotive into commercial service in Scotland, on the Monkland & Kirkintilloch Railway in 1831. They may have been distantly related – both families appear to have originated in north-east England.

Dodd changed the name of the *Argyle* to *Thames*[51] and had her prepared for sea. It appears that an additional mast (which could be lowered) and additional sails were provided, supplementing the existing combined funnel/mast. An advertisement that May offered a marine excursion from the Clyde to the Thames aboard 'the *Thames* schooner, late the *Argyll* steam engine packet'. Nevertheless, most of the voyage south was undertaken under steam, or steam and sail together when the wind was favourable.[52] The *Thames* set off from Glasgow, in mid-May – the limited hours of darkness, at that season, must have been a great help on the many overnight passages that were made. Under command of Captain Dodd was a crew which comprised a mate, four seamen, an engineer, a stoker and a ship's boy. The stoker was kept busy, for the furnace consumed sometimes as much as three tons of coal over 24 hours, and made the lowest part of the funnel too hot to approach.

The *Thames* was too large to pass through the locks of the Forth & Clyde Canal, so the voyage had to be made down the west side of Britain. And an adventurous voyage it proved to be. For a start, when off Portpatrick in a gale, Dodd was able to save the *Thames* from being driven onto a lee shore only by lowering all sail and steaming directly into the wind – a convincing demonstration, if any were needed, of the value of steam power. At Dublin on 28 May he acquired two passengers for London – there do not seem to have been any takers from Glasgow – Mr and Mrs Isaac Weld, and it is to Weld's account, subsequently published, that we owe much of our knowledge of the *Thames* and her voyage[53]. Indeed the description of the furnishings of the main cabin, above, is derived from Weld and describes them presumably as he found them at Dublin – but they seem likely to have been original, since Dodd would scarcely have enhanced them before the sea voyage and indeed would have been more likely to remove things liable to damage.

Weld's account is full of fascinating detail. Off Wexford, and again off St Ives, many small boats set out from shore towards the *Thames* – only to retire again, their occupants cheated of the hopes of right of salvage which they had entertained from a vessel apparently on fire. There were more turbulent conditions encountered, particularly off St Bride's Bay (Pembrokeshire) and Land's End – yet when the boat rolled, and the enclosed sponsons slapped down onto the water one side or the other, they acted immediately as temporary buoyancy to reduce the rolling. One of Captain Dodd's delights was to demonstrate that the steamboat, unlike a sailing vessel, could be steered round in a circle: at the approach to Milford Haven, he encircled the Waterford packet-boat while writing letters to be put aboard, and at Plymouth he ran around warships assembled there. Naval officers were fascinated by the steamboat: several came aboard at Plymouth, and far more – that is, as many as three admirals and eighteen captains – at Portsmouth. Many of them no doubt had already become familiar over several years with the sight of Bentham's steam dredger smokily clearing the channels of Portsmouth harbour, and realised that there was a new power afloat.

Eventually the *Thames* reached Limehouse successfully around 12 June, having travelled, it was calculated, 758 miles with 121½ hours on the move. Her career on the Thames will be mentioned, as with *Margery*'s, in chapter eight. But within days of arrival, Dodd was called to give evidence before the Select Committee of the House of Commons on the Holyhead Roads.[54] The committee's remit covered the whole route between London and Dublin – capital cities in a kingdom recently united – and means to expedite the mails across the Irish Sea were very much part of that remit. It would take a continuing interest in steamboats over the following decade.

SIX

The Forth, the Tay and the Clyde

And what of Henry Bell, and of the *Comet*, while all this was going on? For Bell, as though the problems over the *Glasgow* were not enough, it was in 1814 that William Symington, who had evidently been following events on the Clyde with interest, decided to sue Bell for infringement of his 1801 patent.

This patent was intended to cover any machinery, put in rotative motion by a steam engine, which could be used to drive a boat. Symington's claim for damages was filed that December. Bell's reaction, or rather that of his legal advisors, was not to contest the claim in detail but rather to put in a counter-claim which contested the validity of the patent itself. For once he was well-advised: although the case went to the Court of Session in March 1815, Symington withdrew.[1]

As for the *Comet*, according to Robertson Buchanan she was laid up in the summer of 1814, unable to meet the competition posed by more recent boats of greater power and shallower draft.[2] But this must surely have been only a temporary measure, perhaps representing an interregnum between masters, for in 1814 Bell appointed Robert Bain to be the *Comet*'s master. Bain was then in his mid-twenties. He may be the same Robert Bain who had earlier served Henry Bell as Depute Town Clerk of Helensburgh when Bell was Provost; at any rate he was to prove a loyal servant and supporter of Bell for many years to come.[3] A voyage in 1815 from Glasgow to Greenock by the *Comet* is recorded: unfortunately it took seven hours, of which three were spent aground on a sandbank at Erskine.[4]

In the meantime Henry Bell had become involved in yet another scheme. In 1813 a group of Stirling merchants came together to build a steamboat to ply on the Forth between Stirling and Newhaven, near Edinburgh. On 23 September Bell agreed to 'furnish' them with a 12 hp engine, boiler, paddles and all related equipment, to be of the same quality as the engine and apparatus which he had recently fitted up in the steamboat *Glasgow*. The boat had been ordered from John Gray in Kincardine, and Bell was to supervise construction, fit the engine etc., and maintain it for six months after completion; he was also to provide two engineers, who were to receive the same wages as on the Clyde. In January 1814 it was agreed that the power of the engine should be increased to 15 hp, and two boilers provided. This, it may be deduced, was a reflection of the problems then being experienced with the *Glasgow*. Bell went to Kincardine and supervised construction of the boat and installation of its steam plant. As ever there were additions made to the vessel during construction, and eventually the total sum due to Bell amounted to £1,552,14s 1d, some of which was paid and some disputed.

Meanwhile the owning group had formed itself into the Stirling Steamboat Company; the 'preses', or chairman, was Robert Paterson, who may or may not have been related to Bell's earlier partner of that surname in the Glasgow building trade. Bell became one of the partners and held a one twentieth share.[5]

The boat, named *Stirling*, was launched that spring and started to ply, apparently with success, over her intended route. On the Forth, tides presented greater problems than on the Clyde because of their range, as much as 20 feet in places, their speeds, as much as 14 knots, and a complex pattern of ebb and flow. So *Stirling*'s departure times were varied so that she would be helped by the tides as much as possible and hindered as little as possible.[6]

The proprietors of the steamboat company, or at least a majority of them, then decided to have a second, more powerful, steamboat built. This may have represented a degree of optimism over traffic potential, or perhaps some dissatisfaction with the first boat. The second vessel, the *Lady of the Lake*, 65 feet over the keel and with a 20 hp engine, went into service in 1815. But in the event there proved to be insufficient traffic for two boats and the position must have been aggravated by the appearance the same season of the steamboat *Morning Star*, which started to ply on the Forth between Alloa and Leith.[7]

The reaction of the steamboat company was to put *Stirling* up for sale. But Henry Bell had sufficient confidence in the boat to agree to buy her himself, for £1,200 payable in monthly instalments of £50; possession of the boat passed to him on the occasion of the initial payment. What Bell then did was to pay up until the instalments totalled £500 – that is, until the sum still due from him was equivalent to the sum which he considered the steamboat company still owed him. He then stopped paying. Not unreasonable, one might think, but the steamboat company thought otherwise and took him to court. The case rumbled on until 1818. It then went against Bell, apparently on the grounds that two separate deals were involved and they should be treated separately.[8] But Bell had possession of the *Stirling* and was operating her.

He did more. In 1816, he brought the *Comet* herself back to the Forth. There she operated between Newhaven and Grangemouth, the entrance to the Forth & Clyde Canal, where she connected with the canal passage boats to provide a service between Edinburgh and Glasgow.[9] This was several years before the Edinburgh & Glasgow Union Canal was opened to complete a wholly-canal route between the two cities.

Early in 1817 Bell was promoting a scheme for a regular service for freight between Leith, Grangemouth, Glasgow, Bowling and Greenock, using steamboats to tow lighters along the firths of Forth and Clyde, lighters which would be tracked by horses along the canal section of the route.[10] As we have seen, use of steamboats to tow lighters in this way is unlikely to have been the wholly original concept that he would probably have liked people to suppose, and any hopes he may have had towards benefitting financially from the proposal seem not to have come to fruition. But that May, at Wood's Port Glasgow yard, the steamboat *Tug* was launched for the Edinburgh, Glasgow & Leith Shipping Co. She was 73 feet long overall and equipped with two 16 hp engines from Duncan McArthur & Co.: too long to pass through the Forth & Clyde Canal locks, but powerful enough to make her way from the Clyde round the north of Scotland to the Forth. There she took up her appointed task of towing purpose-built lighters between Leith and the canal, and carrying some passengers too.[11] It was from the steamboat *Tug* that the familiar generic use of the term 'tug' for this type of craft originated.

From this period onward use of steamboats became commonplace on the Forth, both up and down the firth and, from the early 1820s, on the ferries across it. But Henry Bell, ever the schemer, was soon looking further afield. Before following that part of the story it is necessary, however, to see what was happening nearer home, firstly and briefly on the Firth of Tay, and then at greater length on the Clyde.

Robertson and the Firth of Tay

Henry Bell was not alone among the pioneers of the *Comet* in looking towards the east coast as well as the west. In 1814 John Robertson, not content with putting the steamboat *Clyde* into service on the Firth of Clyde, put the steamboat *Tay* into service on the Firth of Tay. The boat, some 60 feet long, was built for him by J. Smart of Dundee, and Robertson himself provided the engine. Robertson had family links with Perthshire, and the *Tay* went into service between Dundee and Perth on 4 April. The voyage took three hours and she ran regularly until 1818. Robertson then moved her to the Clyde, possibly because the service was uneconomic, but at any rate she was soon replaced, and a regular year-round steamboat service for passengers and goods was maintained between Perth and Dundee until the Dundee & Perth Railway was opened in 1847.[12]

Robertson had two more steamboats built for him on the Tay, the *Caledonia* and the *Humber*. Both were probably built by Smart, with engines by Robertson, and both were built for service on the Humber. The *Caledonia* was completed first, and was the first Scottish-built steamboat to go south under her own steam. She left in the late summer of 1814 with Robertson on board. It was an adventurous voyage: caught in a strong gale which carried away the paddle boxes and much else, she had to run for shelter in the Tyne, and only succeeded in surmounting the breakers on the bar at its mouth by taking shelter under the lee of a large collier which was also making for harbour. She eventually reached the Humber, and appears to have gone into service between Hull and Gainsborough, on the Trent, that October. *Humber* followed later and went into service between Hull and Selby, on the Ouse.[13] The further story of steamboat services on these rivers is taken up in chapter eight.

A few years later, the Tay saw further steamboat innovation. The ferries across the Firth of Tay had ever been important, and in 1819 an Act of Parliament authorised trustees to improve the Dundee–Tayport crossing. Robert Stevenson, of lighthouse fame, drew up plans for improved piers and so on, but funds were lacking to put them into effect. The solution was a loan from the Exchequer Bill Loan Commissioners, a government body which was providing loans for public works to relieve distress during the depression which followed the end of the Napoleonic wars. Their adviser on all things involving civil engineering was Thomas Telford. Telford modified the Tay ferry proposals and crossed swords with Stevenson in the process, but it was Telford's final plans which were put into effect. Sloping masonry slips, able to accommodate a ferryboat whatever the state of the tide, were built on both shores, that on the north side being 150 yards long. From 1821, these were being linked by the steamboat *Union*; a second, similar, boat was added a couple of years later, and a third later still.

These were remarkable innovative vessels, 'twin boats' or catamarans, with a single paddle wheel centrally placed between the hulls. The second boat certainly, and the third possibly, were bi-directional, with rudders at both ends. The machinery was built by noted Dundee engineers J. & C. Carmichael. They were about 92 feet long and 34 feet in beam, with plenty of room for passengers, cattle and horses, and carriages and carts, which were driven on and off without unhitching the horses. For many years they provided an important service across the firth.[14]

Similar double-ended steam ferry boats were introduced successfully in 1822–3 on the very old-established ferry across the Forth at Alloa.[15]

Expansion on the Clyde

On the Clyde, 1815 and the years which followed were years of rapid expansion, both of steamboat routes and of the quantity of steamboats needed to serve them. To the early destinations, from Glasgow, of Greenock, Gourock, Helensburgh and Largs were soon added Dumbarton, Rothesay, Ayr, Brodick, Campbeltown, Inverary, Arrochar and places in between. Inverary was a particular goal, both by water throughout via the Kyles of Bute and Lochgilphead, and via Loch Long and Loch Goil to Lochgoilhead, whence Inverary was not too far away by land, or by ferry over Loch Fyne.

Between 1815 and 1819, according to Williamson, twenty-six steamers were built on the Clyde.[16] During this period John Wood & Co. alone built eleven.[17] Not all of these were for service on the Clyde, for use of steamboats was already spreading far and wide, but many of them were. And subsequently the pace showed no sign of slackening.

There were some noteworthy vessels built for the Clyde and its associated lochs at this period. David Napier entered the shipowning business in 1816 with the *Marion*. She was built for him by MacLachlan at Dumbarton; he himself provided the machinery, and named his boat after Mrs Napier. The *Marion* was not large and, after a season on the Clyde, Napier in 1817 took her up the River Leven to Loch Lomond.[18] There she started the tradition of paddle-steamer services on the loch which continued unbroken until the withdrawal of *Maid of the Loch* in 1981, and which seems likely to be resumed before too long with the return to service of the *Maid of the Loch* restored.

Of the other *Comet* pioneers, John Robertson opened up the Lochgoilhead route with the *Defiance*, built for him by Wood in 1817; evidently this was a success, for he then brought the *Tay* to the Clyde, re-named her *Oscar*, and set her to work on the same route. The following year he had the *Marquis of Bute* built by Wood for the Glasgow–Gourock run. All these operations were profitable and Robertson became for a while a rich man, only for his fortune to ebb away again later.[19]

The *Caledonia*, built by Wood in 1815 with engines by Greenhead Foundry Co.,[20] went south a year or two later and was bought by James Watt junior to become in effect a floating test bed for Boulton, Watt & Co. as described in chapter eight. The *Post Boy*, built by William Denny at Dumbarton in 1820 with an engine by David Napier, was the first steamer advertised to depart from Glasgow at a set hour irrespective of wind or tide. That she could do so was a consequence of shallow draft – 3 feet – and increasing improvements to the river itself. She sailed at 6.00 a.m. and was thus able to make a connection at Dumbarton for coaches to Balloch, which in turn connected with the *Marion*.[21] The *Leven*, built at Dumbarton in 1823, was fitted with a side-lever engine by Robert Napier, the first he built. Robert Napier, younger cousin and also brother-in-law of David Napier, was then in the early stages of an engineering career which would eventually see him one of the most distinguished of Clyde shipbuilders – 'the parent and patriarch of modern engineering and shipbuilding', Williamson called him in 1904.[22]

In 1825, there were thirty-nine passenger steamers serving Clyde destinations from Glasgow. This includes two on Loch Lomond, but excludes those already travelling beyond the Clyde, to the West Highlands, to Liverpool and to Belfast, as will be described in chapters seven and nine. There were also six 'luggage boats' (such as *Industry* and her like) and three tugs. So the total was forty-eight steamboats[23] of one sort or another, none of which had been there a mere fourteen years before – or even imagined, by most people apart from visionary schemers. By this date, though, the increase was evidently levelling off, for comparable numbers quoted for 1831 and 1835 are forty-three and forty-nine respectively.[24]

Typically, such vessels were owned by syndicates of businessmen keen to improve communications with their home town. The Dumbarton Steamboat Company, for instance, had been formed in 1815 by shipbuilder James Lang, his brother Alexander Lang who was a grocer, and ship's carpenter William Latta, who was married to James Lang's niece. Their first vessel was the *Duke of Wellington*, memories of Waterloo being recent.[25]

The crew of a steamboat in the early period typically comprised: captain, pilot (whose task was to steer), two enginemen, a seaman and his assistant, and a steward and his assistant, totalling eight in number.[26] Sometimes, the captain was one of the owning syndicate. Many captains are said to have come from land-based occupations – schoolmasters, carriers and so on[27] – and clearly, with a new technology expanding rapidly, there was inevitably a shortage of men with experience. There is a strange story, repeated down the years, of how the engineer of the *Dumbarton Castle* in 1816 did not know how to reverse the engine – until this was explained to him by James Watt in person. Watt was a passenger on board, making what would be his last visit to Greenock, and had naturally fallen into conversation with the engineer. The latter remarked on how, as an interesting phenomenon, when the vessel had been aground, the pressure put on the paddle floats by the rising tide had caused the wheels to rotate backwards and the engine to reverse. His usual practice when approaching a quay had been to stop the engine and let the boat drift in to land. It sounds as though the engine was fitted with slip eccentrics, in which case, as long as the boat had any way on it, pressure of water on the floats would have made it difficult to reverse. At any rate, safely moored alongside Rothesay quay, Watt was able to demonstrate how it should be done.[28]

Nevertheless, steamboat travel was reliable enough, and cheap enough and fast enough to attract passengers in huge numbers. Before there were steamboats, according to Cleland in 1816, passage boats, or fly boats, carried not more than fifty persons from Glasgow to Greenock in the day, and as many back again, while road coaches carried perhaps twenty-four people in each direction. Since steamboats had been introduced, the total number had increased to four or five hundred.[29] George Dodd, a couple of years later, put the figures at eighty, and 4–600. They enjoyed, he enthused, 'the healthful amusement of a water excursion, and the enchanting beauties of the Clyde'.[30] Its banks were, in those days, still largely rural. There were, of course, hazards. Some of these were occasional, such as the south-westerly gale of 17 November 1814, so strong that a steamboat, carrying sail, was dismasted – or, if it is not over-ingenious to suggest it, dis-funneled, since mast and funnel were identical. Her passengers were taken on board by a second steamboat which, despite the delay, and encouraged no doubt by the gale, still reached Glasgow in three hours from Greenock.[31] A more regular hazard was the lack of piers at many of the calling places. There were quays at Glasgow's Broomielaw, Port Glasgow, Greenock, Rothesay (apparently since mediaeval times), and a few other places. But at most points of call passengers had to be put aboard and landed by small boats from the shore,[32] with all the discomfort and danger that implied. At Helensburgh itself, the first rough pier was built only in 1816.[33] Safety was improved when in that same year Glasgow Magistrates and Council, in their capacity as navigation trustees, enacted regulations for steamboats. One of these was to the effect that while passengers, or goods, were being taken on board or landed by small boats, the paddles of the steamboat itself must be stopped. Points covered by other regulations included reservation of part of the Broomielaw quay for steamboats, safety measures when steamboats passed or overtook one another, and a requirement for lights and lookouts when on the move after dark.[34]

The overwhelming success of steamboats meant that traffic by coach along the shores of the Clyde was largely superseded; coaches ceased to run.[35] The mails for Greenock were carried by steamboat.[36] The towing path, so recently built alongside the upper part of the Clyde, was abandoned as such in 1825, although it may have continued in use for a time.[37] Improvements continued to the navigation itself, particularly after the belated introduction of the steam dredger in 1824. By 1834 vessels drawing as much as 13 feet were able to reach Glasgow on spring tides, and by 1845 the figure had reached 18 feet.[38]

Not all of the passenger traffic originated at Glasgow, however. Inhabitants of the Highland regions north-west of the firth were also quick to make steamboat travel part of their daily lives. A good taste of this is given in one of the journals of Dorothy Wordsworth, sister of the poet. She and a travelling companion, touring Scotland, voyaged by steamboat from Inverary to Glasgow on 24 September 1822; they were on board at Inverary by 5 a.m., taking their places not in the 'gentry end' but, as was their custom, in the steerage at the fore end of the boat. At first this was almost empty, but at Ardrishaig:

> We take in passengers and luggage … chiefly peasantry – the women look anxiously till their panniers are stowed, or, fancying the important charge less endangered in their own care, they descend with their burthens – baskets of eggs, fowls, etc … our end of the vessel is now pretty well covered with people and their luggage. Bundles of all sorts and sizes – a lot of chickens, tyed [sic] by the legs, is lying at my feet … The mountain island of Arran, beautiful in form and outline, soft as a cloud yet perfectly distinct, is before us … Not a boat now moving on the wide expanse of calm water … but ours, which sends its black rolling fleeces over the gentry's heads, while the sky above our end of the boat is a bright clear blue. I sit aloft on a bundle … my neighbours two women who can hardly speak twenty words of English. [ie they were talking in Gaelic.] An old man with a huge hamper of chickens is going to Greenock. I hear him say

that he had walked twenty miles this morning with that burthen before he took boat at Tarbet … It is his business to travel from house to house in the Highlands, picking up fowls and eggs and any other marketable commodities.

And at Greenock many of the Highlanders:

…depart with their hampers, baskets and bundles. A big-boned porter greets a bare-headed and bare-footed girl, whose charge has been a weighty basket of eggs, with 'God bless thy bonny face', and lifting up her load hies with it over the plank and she follows him. Boys and men, the moment we drew under the wall, hurried onboard with apples, pears and cakes to sell; and shops of eatables on the shore were innumerable … At the sound of the horn, passengers, who had landed, hurried back to the boat, and the hawkers were off with their stores. The sail from Greenock to Port Glasgow, as delightful as glorious prospects of mountains and gently-varied shores could make it…

She landed at Glasgow in the twilight.[39]

So the steamboat passengers on the Clyde comprised not only Glaswegians on their way to and from the coast, but Highlanders on their way to and from Greenock and Glasgow. To these, from the 1820s onwards, were added, in rapidly increasing numbers, tourists from further afield – from England, and from the Continent – in search of the picturesque. In their search they were aided by guidebooks such as Lumsden & Sons' *The Steamboat Companion…*, first published in 1820 and frequently re-issued. None of these people had known anything of steamboats a decade or two earlier. Steamboat travel had burst upon the public consciousness with all the suddenness of electronic communications in our own day, and had been embraced with the same all-pervading enthusiasm.

Adding to the traffic was what one writer in 1822 referred to as the growing addiction of families from the 'mercantile and professional classes' to a summer by the sea, at such distance from the city as would allow the head of the family to return to work during the week. This could mean taking rooms in an established household – it was noted in the mid-1830s that more than half of Helensburgh's 126 households took in lodgers.[40] Or it could mean taking an entire house – even though these might leave something to be desired. Here, from an account of 1822, is what the narrator thought of the Helensburgh house which his friends had taken for the summer:

It was one of the thackit [i.e., thatched] houses near the burn – a very sweet place, to be sure, of its kind; but … both damp and vastly inconvenient. The floor of the best room was clay, and to cover the naked walls they had brought carpets from home, which they hung around them like curtains … Mrs M'Waft … got out the wine and the glasses, and a loaf of bread, that was blue moulded, from the damp of the house; and I said to her, 'that surely the cause which had such effect on the bread, must be of some consequence to the body.' 'But the sea and country air,' replied Mr M'Waft, 'makes up for more than all such sort of inconveniences.'[41]

This of course is gentle satire, although perhaps not so exaggerated as might be supposed, given the general standard of housing in the Highlands during that period. To be fair to Helensburgh, by this date rows of two-storey houses had already been built, and mansions were starting to appear.[42] The pier was improved in the 1830s.

The real mark of success for the Glasgow merchant was to possess his own seaside villa, to be reached by steamboat. This meant building both villas and piers at which the steamboats could call. David Napier was to the fore in this movement. In 1828 he purchased an extensive tract of land along the north shore of Holy Loch, an area inaccessible by road but containing the clachan of Kilmun, which then comprised an ancient church and a few cottages. He built a pier, which was served by his own steamers, and added workmens' houses, some substantial villas, a hotel and roads. 'Houses to let, ground to feu', he advertised in 1829; villas and houses eventually extended along the shore for three miles or so, from Kilmun to Blairmore, and two more piers were built.[43]

Dunoon has been conspicuous by its absence so far from the places mentioned as being served by steamers. But Dunoon also, as late as 1822, was no more than a Highland clachan, with only three or four slate-roofed houses, a parish church and a manse. Then, when steamboats started to venture across the firth, a few families started to come to Dunoon for the summer. Wealthy men started to build villas, those still wealthier to buy estates in the neighbourhood. But people still had to disembark from the steamers, or join them, by small open boats. It was not until as late as 1835 that a company was formed to build a pier at Dunoon, which it did successfully.[44] Piers were gradually added elsewhere on the Firth of Clyde throughout the 1830s, 1840s and 1850s.

Such stories of development, consequent on the establishment of steamer services, would be repeated again and again at places on the shore of the firth, and particularly on the north-west or Highland side.[45]

In 1837 it was stated that 692,000 passengers travelled by river from Glasgow to Greenock and beyond.[46] This first era of Clyde steamer services, during which they were immensely popular, immensely busy and unchallenged by other forms of transport, reached its zenith in 1840. In 1841 there was opened the Glasgow, Paisley & Greenock Railway, one of the earliest steam passenger railways in Scotland. But whereas construction of railways elsewhere had a calamitous effect on coach services between the places served, the interaction between this railway and Clyde steamboat services was, at least initially, far more equivocal. Although promoters of the railway had anticipated that steamboat proprietors would alter their services so as to connect with trains at Greenock, many of the proprietors preferred not to do so, and the railway company was reduced, for a while, to chartering its own boats. Many steamboat passengers, it seems, preferred a through journey and a conveniently located quay at the Broomielaw to an awkward interchange at Greenock and a comparatively inconvenient railway terminus at Bridge Street, Glasgow – despite a saving in journey time by train.[47] An awkward sort of *modus vivendi*, of varied competition and co-operation, between rail and steamer seems to have ensued over several decades. Meanwhile the railway system expanded, but the topography of the Highland side of the firth, deeply indented by sea lochs among high mountains, prevented construction of railways there. Eventually, in the 1880s and 1890s, most of the steamer services to places on its shores came to be operated by railway companies, the steamers running in connection with trains as extensions of the railway system in a network which became famed far and wide for its efficiency.

This remained the basic situation until the 1960s. But that rugged terrain which had prevented construction of railways to places north and west of the Firth of Clyde was not so severe as to prevent construction of new motor roads. At that period, with roads and motor vehicles very much in the ascendant, longitudinal services by steamer and motor vessel up and down the firth were successively withdrawn, to be replaced by vehicle ferries traversing the shortest crossings. That situation persists at the present day. Since the emphasis now is not so much on the motor car as on modal shift away from it, it seems time for transport planners to revisit the neglected potential for passenger transport that is represented by the Clyde.

SEVEN

The Way to Inverness –
Bell's Last Great Scheme

Just what drew the attention of Henry Bell to the Caledonian Canal and its potential for steamboat travel is uncertain. It would, of course, have been difficult for anyone around 1812 to have been unaware of its construction. It was as yet incomplete – its colossal scale was mentioned in chapter two – and such a large waterway was inevitably a long time building.

It was made even longer by the equivocal attitude of one of the principal landowners on the route. He was Macdonell of Glengarry, whose tartan-clad portrait by Raeburn is familiar from innumerable shortbread tins. Glengarry's character was of a complexity to exceed that of Henry Bell himself. He was able both to promote the trappings of his Gaelic heritage, and to clear his crofters in favour of sheep farmers. He was able to welcome the Caledonian Canal as 'this Great National Work', but to resist its actual construction, at one stage by force. His lawsuits with the canal commissioners would continue for years.[1]

In the summer of 1818, however, the canal section from the Beauly Firth up to Loch Ness was opened, and although there were subsequently some temporary closures for finishing works, it was becoming clear that completion of the canal would not be too long delayed. But the Great Glen is a long way from Helensburgh, and further still from the Firth of Forth, where Bell's steamboats were based at this period. How did he become aware of this? The *Tug* arrived on the Forth in 1817, after a delivery voyage from her Clyde builder made, of necessity, round the north of Scotland. This may have drawn attention to the potential of a coast-to-coast canal, with locks substantially larger than those of the Forth & Clyde. More specifically,

Telford's resident engineer for construction of the western section of the Caledonian Canal was Alexander Easton. As mentioned in chapter three, he appears to have been a kinsman of Bell's through Bell's mother, Margaret Easton. It seems very likely that the two men were in touch, although nothing has emerged during research for this book to confirm whether this was so. But Bell was evidently well-enough informed of the canal's progress to home in on it as a steamer route to match his entrepreneurial spirit, in preference to other routes closer to home. And those responsible for the canal seem to have been remarkably well-informed of steamboat progress from a very early date.

As early as October 1813, Telford himself wrote, in his regular report to the Caledonian Canal Commissioners and with reference to Loch Oich:

> With a view to facilitating the passage of Vessels along this narrow Lake, it was originally proposed to provide a Towing Path so that in a Calm, or contrary winds, they might be hauled by Horses; but the success with which Steam Boats have been for some years past, employed upon the River Clyde between Glasgow and Greenock, affords good reason to expect that not only upon this Lake, but upon the whole length of the Canal Navigation (together Twenty Seven Miles) the use of Horses may be dispensed with, and that the sundry Steam Engines now in the possession of the Commissioners, may be profitably substituted.[2]

The steam engines to which he referred were pumps, and it did not in fact prove possible to re-use them to power tugs, as Telford appeared to envisage. But the proposed towpath along the south-eastern shore of Loch Oich was not made, and instead a navigation channel was eventually dredged down the middle of it – much to the fury of Glengarry, whose mansion house stood on the north-western shore, and who regarded the loch as part of his pleasure grounds.

Redundancy of the towpath, however, would prove to be a minor issue among the consequences for the Caledonian Canal of the development of steamboats and steamships. The very purpose itself of the canal was largely negated, for the passage round the north of Scotland became far less of a problem to steamers than it had been to sailing ships. Yet the course of history is sometimes strange: remarkably, it would be the same individual, Henry Bell, who was responsible for the introduction of steamboats, who would also, at least in part, alleviate the canal's problems by demonstrating its value as a route for them.

The Crinan Canal, opened in 1801, was the key to the water route between Glasgow, the West Highlands and western entrance to the Caledonian Canal. It enabled small ships to avoid the long and dangerous passage round the Mull of Kintyre by crossing Knapdale between Ardrishaig and Crinan. It was the property of the Crinan Canal Company, an impecunious undertaking, and in 1816 the canal itself, in poor condition, had been placed under the control of the Caledonian Canal Commissioners so that public money could be used to bring it up to an adequate standard. The canal's resident engineer since 1814 had been William Thomson: he continued in post. He had been acquainted with Henry Bell during the period when the *Comet* was being built and put into service, and in 1818 the acquaintanceship was renewed. The two men corresponded with one another over the extension of steam boat services from the Clyde through the canal and to the West Highlands: Thomson considered that it would be beneficial to the Highlands and remunerative to the operator. Specifically, it appears that he was willing to allow *Comet* to pass through the Crinan Canal free of charge.[3]

Bell's first step in bringing steamboat services to the West Highlands and the Caledonian Canal was to put *Comet* into service between Glasgow and Fort William. But *Comet* was a very small vessel for such a service, for although much of the route beyond Crinan is sheltered from most points of the compass, it is exposed to the south-west whence the prevailing winds come. As a preliminary, it was necessary to lengthen *Comet*. The work was done in 1819, on the beach at Helensburgh: that has caused comment down the years, but bearing in mind that at this period most shipbuilding was done on the foreshore, it is not perhaps working on the beach which is a surprise but the absence of an established shipyard. But Bell was evidently on hand to supervise, and the work was done by James Nicol. There was a noted boatbuilding family called Nicol based in Greenock at this period. Authorities old and recent have differed about how many times during the course of her career the *Comet* was lengthened, and by how much. However, her original registration certificate of 1813 was not cancelled until 10 February 1820; on the same day she was re-registered 'on account of an increase in the dimensions'. The new certificate gave her length 'from the Fore-part of the Main Stem to the After-part of the Stern Post aloft' as 73 feet 10 inches.[4]

This longer vessel evidently demanded a more powerful engine. The original engine was taken out while she was being rebuilt, and sold for further use on land; a new 6 hp engine, made in Greenock, was installed.[5] Probably this was soon matched by a new boiler – at least, in December

1819 Bell wrote in his inimitable fashion: 'I am going to give her a new sett of boilars.'[6]

The lengthening work was completed in time for Bell to advertise that *Comet* would start to ply between Glasgow and Fort William on 2 September 1819, northbound from Glasgow on Thursdays and southbound from Fort William on Mondays. Calls en route were at Greenock, Gourock, Rothesay, Tarbet, Lochgilp, Crinan, Easdale, Oban and Port Appin. Fares ranged from 2s 6d, Glasgow–Greenock in steerage, to 22s 0d, Glasgow–Fort William in cabin.[7] This programme she appears to have followed until December, by which date passengers were too few and storms too severe to continue through the winter.[8]

Although things were going satisfactorily for Bell in the west, all was not well in the east. Early in the summer of 1819, while the *Stirling* was in Grangemouth harbour, her boiler exploded. Despite the earlier intention to fit two boilers, there seems to have been only one and it was made, wholly or in part, of cast iron. Her engine room, too, was single-manned. By this date most steamboats on both the Forth and the Clyde had boilers of wrought iron or copper which, though they might burst, would not shatter, and employed an engineer to mind the engine and a fireman to stoke the boiler. The *Stirling* was interdicted from plying on the Forth until 'it shall be ascertained, by the examination of persons of skill, that the boiler shall have been so constructed or repaired as that it may be navigated with safety'.[9]

The work must have been done to the satisfaction of the 'persons of skill', for early in April 1820 Bell was not only advertising the services offered by both *Comet* and *Stirling* but pointing out that people could conveniently connect through from Edinburgh to Fort William by combining both steamboats with the passage boats on the Forth & Clyde Canal.[10]

By then, perhaps inevitably, Bell's vision for the west was soaring far and wide beyond the actual route he was operating. He was envisaging schemes for steamboat services up the coast and to the islands, even as far as the Outer Hebrides. For these he perceived that support would be needed not so much from the mercantile class which had backed steamboats on the Clyde, but from the great landowners of the region. He corresponded with them, attempting to arouse their interest, not without some success.[11]

The steamboat *Highland Chieftain* made a trial voyage up the coast as far as Skye that summer. Bell appears not to have been one of her shareholders at this stage, although he became one later. The *Highland Chieftain* had started life as the *Duke of Wellington*, built in 1817 at Dumbarton for the up-river route to Glasgow: she had been enlarged and repaired before setting out for Skye.[12] Services built up gradually – by the end of the 1820s steamboats were taking tourists to, for instance, Staffa, Iona, Mull, Skye and Lewis. Equally, steamboats entered Gaelic culture as the means which the islanders adopted when they needed to leave home for the Lowlands.[13] As things turned out, these services were developed by other entrepreneurs, rather than by Bell.

But it was from Henry Bell's initial vision that there eventually emerged in Victorian times the comprehensive coastal steamer services which linked Glasgow with the West Highlands and the Islands, and each of these with the others,[14] and which became inextricably linked with the name 'MacBrayne'. By the 1930s MacBraynes were developing into a multi-modal transport service for the region, operating buses for passengers and lorries for freight, as well as ships: but after nationalisation, transport was divided up according to mode rather than need, and West Highland shipping services were largely reduced, as on the Clyde, to vehicle ferries, in this case by the shortest routes between mainland and islands.

Back in 1819–20, it appears that Bell with the *Comet*, of which he was sole owner, had become out of step with the multiple ownership of other steamboats, most if not all of which belonged to syndicates. He divided ownership of the vessel into thirty-six shares and started to sell these off. They went well, among both West Highland landowners and Fort William merchants. It is a fair guess that Bell initially intended to keep some shares in the *Comet* for himself, but if so the prospect of good money coming in was too much for him, and by the end of the summer he had sold the lot. The resulting syndicate became the Comet Steam Boat Company, and in September the shareholders elected a committee, to take effect from the following 1 January. Henry Bell featured on it as 'Superintendent'. Sales of shares must have been aided by the visible success that summer of the service provided: on 3 August, for instance, *Comet* sailed from Glasgow with as many as 155 passengers on board.[15] By the autumn Bell was making arrangements for a new and more powerful boat to be built.[16]

Glasgow to Fort William was not, though, the full extent of the route which Bell was seeking to open up. In their seventeenth annual report, dated 25 May 1820, the Caledonian Canal Commissioners noted the regular arrival of a steamboat at Fort William from Glasgow, 'having obtained permission to pass through the Crinan Canal', and added that 'an application has recently been received to navigate the Caledonian Canal from the Beauley Frith [*sic*] to Loch-Ness in like manner'. They were 'disposed to afford facility and encouragement to this mode of Travelling, which … tends to the improvement of the Highlands of Scotland'.[17] They did not say whom the applicant might be but the following November, in the engineer's report on the state of the canal (which was printed as an appendix to the eighteenth annual report), Thomas Telford himself enthused:

> During the present season ... the ingenious and enterprising Mr. Henry Bell, the inventor of Steam Boats, (and by whose exertions the first conveyance of that kind was put in motion on both the Rivers Clyde and Forth,) has established one which plies between the [head of] Muirtown Locks [Inverness] and Fort Augustus; it is 68 feet in length, and (including the Paddle Cases) 23 feet in breadth, and is worked by an engine of 18 Horse Power; during the summer Months it went and returned in the same day; at present it goes up one day and returns the next ... Passengers ... have been comparatively numerous, considering the limited range yet opened. From Fort Augustus, a *Diligence*, carrying four insides and three outsides, proceeds to Fort William, where another Steam Boat conveys the Passengers down the Linnhè-Loch by the Crinan Canal to Greenock and Glasgow. This latter, by having a more extended connexion, and being the second year of its performance, has been proportionally more productive, which has induced the Proprietors to construct another for the same line of conveyance; so that when there is a Water-Passage across the Island, in all probability the great line of intercourse between the Southern and Northern parts of Scotland, as well as from the North of England and Ireland will be through this valley of the Caledonian Canal, the *Great Glen* of Scotland.[18]

The steamboat was the *Stirling* or, as she must now be called, the *Stirling Castle* – her name was changed, apparently at this point in her career.[19] As with the *Comet*, Bell was funding her by selling shares – he was presumably paying off a new boiler and perhaps, in view of the increased figure for horsepower, a replacement engine. One of the shareholders was Duncan McArthur, who may well have been the engine-builder of that name. Thomas Telford himself was a shareholder, and so was one of his right-hand men, John Mitchell.[20] John Mitchell was Chief Inspector and Superintendent of Highland Roads and Bridges: throughout the period that the Caledonian Canal had been building, a second set of Parliamentary commissioners, also with Telford as their engineer, had been building roads and bridges in the Highlands. Mitchell as their chief inspector had grown to be a man greatly respected throughout the region, particularly by the landowners, who had a substantial financial responsibility for the roads and bridges which he superintended. Both men were valuable allies for Bell.

By December 1820 it must have seemed to Henry Bell that his affairs were at last going really well. Then, disaster struck. On 15 December *Comet*, on her way south from Fort William to Glasgow, was wrecked.

The location was Craignish Point. This point remains well-known to this day to west coast yachtsmen, but is scarcely known at all to anyone else. It is the tip of the Craignish peninsula, which itself projects south south-west from the coast of Lorne. To landsmen, it is a remote spot. The single-track road down the peninsula gives out a mile short of the point, at a derelict pier at Aird. From here, in days gone by, there was a ferry to the northern end of the Isle of Jura. And MacBrayne's coastwise steamer, following the route pioneered by Bell, would wait off-shore while passengers were brought out to her, or landed, by ferry boat. But all that is now in the past. Beyond the road-end lies only rocky, rugged moorland, interspersed with little hills and patches of bog, contained within a rocky shore.

To mariners, however, Craignish Point is a prominent feature of this coast. Any vessel coming from Crinan and heading northwards towards Oban has to round it. And about one third of a mile offshore lies the island of Garbh Rèisa, first and largest of a chain of isles, islets and rocks which continues the line of the peninsula far down the Sound of Jura. This gap of one third of a mile is the Dorus Mór, the Great Gate: safe enough, but only given good weather, and favourable winds and tides. The tides run strongly here.

A little hill, a quarter-mile or so short of the point itself, provides in fine weather an excellent vantage place, from which the significance of Craignish Point can be appreciated. To the south-east, a little over three miles away across the mouth of Loch Craignish, the white-painted buildings of Crinan stand out. Close in front is the Dorus Mór, a watery gateway between the heights of point and island. Far away to the south-west, the distinctive shape of the mountains called the Paps of Jura can be discerned. Closer at hand, and to the west, is the strait between the Isles of Jura and Scarba called the Gulf of Corrievreckan, with its notorious whirlpool. And, after you have turned through more than 180 degrees from the original direction, the long, low outline of the Isle of Luing can be seen away to the north-west; behind it, that is between it and Scarba, lies the Sound of Luing, the route to Oban and the North.

The weather was not good on 15 December 1820. *Comet* had spent the previous night at Oban, with men pumping, apparently continuously, consequent on an earlier encounter with a rock. But nevertheless she set out southwards, in a snowstorm with a strong wind from the east. Bell himself was on board, returning from Fort William where he had been gathering support for the new, larger ship. One can imagine *Comet*, wallowing southwards, as she approached Craignish after 4.00 p.m. – it must already have been dusk, if not dark. Probably she kept close in to the shoreline, for maximum protection from the wind, and to keep well clear of Corrievreckan; perhaps she was even closer than those on board realised. At any rate, when she rounded the point about 4.30 p.m. she caught the full force of the gale, and this, and a strong tide, forced her bow so far round that she immediately ran among the rocks. Maybe, with her bilges already full of water, she was slow to answer the helm when attempts were made to put her back on course. One account states that a strong gust laid her on her beam ends. This seems unlikely, for in that case she would presumably have been blown ashore broadside on, more or less; in fact, she seems more likely to have been under power at the moment of impact, for her bow was driven so far up among the rocks that those on board were able to land without apparent difficulty, and the forward part of the ship remained sufficiently intact for much effort to be put in over the next ten days to salvage equipment and materials from the wreck. The aft part of the ship, however, broke off at the point at which it had previously been lengthened, and floated off towards the Gulf of Corrievreckan.[21]

There are many questions of detail, to which one would like to know the answer, but probably never will. Why so late in the afternoon, at that season? Had the start been delayed by the weather? Or had the voyage, because of the condition of the ship, just taken longer than anticipated, to be overtaken by nightfall? Or had the timing simply been dictated by the tides? And what happened to those on board once they had got ashore? The nearest habitation today is a long mile away, although in the 1820s there might have been crofts nearer the point. So did someone set out with a lantern across trackless, rugged country in the dark to seek help? Or did they simply huddle together on the shore through a long, cold December night, until daybreak enabled the wreck to be spied from Crinan, and rescue came? One thing sadly remains clear: when *Comet* was wrecked on that December evening, she was no more than three miles or so short of Crinan and safety.

The salvage attempts were made, of necessity in this remote location, by boat: an account book, which survives, details payments for hire of boats, for men working at Craignish until 25 December, and for purchase of a substantial amount of whisky with which to encourage them. From 23 to 25 December two large boats were present while the men tried to recover the engine. They were not wholly successful, and only parts of the machinery were saved.[22]

The new steamboat, already planned by the Comet Steamboat Company, was built by James Lang at Dumbarton – the first of many steamboats to be built at a yard which had earlier built large, ocean-going sailing ships. She was 81 feet long. The engine was supplied by Duncan McArthur and is variously said to have been of 25 or 30 hp; the boiler was of copper. The name *Comet* was re-used: no doubt a good marketing move, but one which led to much confusion between the two vessels.[23] Recent writers have tended to use the style *Comet II*, but this does not appear to have been used by contemporaries of the vessel herself.

The second *Comet* was ready in time to enter service on 6 July 1821; in the interim, *Highland Chieftain* had been plying between Glasgow and Fort William.[24] On the eastern part of the Caledonian Canal the *Stirling Castle*, which had ceased running on 23 December 1820, started up again on 5 April. By the late summer the western end of the Caledonian Canal was complete enough for the second *Comet* to venture on to it. She went from Corpach up Neptune's Staircase and as far as the eastern end of Loch Lochy, some twenty miles, and back again. This occasion was in the nature of a gala day, with the canal officials showing off the canal to the local gentry. Also lucky enough to be on board was a seventeen-year old lad, who was gaining practical training as an engineer by working on the locks being built at Fort Augustus. He was Joseph Mitchell, son of John, who had ahead of him a long and distinguished career as an engineer of roads and, eventually, railways in the Highlands – although he is perhaps better remembered today for his *Reminiscences...*, written in old age, which offer a window onto Highland life and society in the first part of the nineteenth century. To that seventeen-year old, the steamboat was a novelty and a wonder, the trip very enjoyable.[25]

At long last, in their annual report of May 1822, the Caledonian Canal Commissioners were able to state that their canal had, since the previous October, been open for traffic – not yet to the full intended depth, but open nonetheless, no small achievement for a project so vast that many had doubted that it would ever be completed.[26]

The opening of the canal throughout was marked by a cruise from Inverness right through to Fort William and back again, on 23–5 October 1821. The vessel used was the *Stirling Castle*, hired for the purpose by the canal commissioners at a cost of £69 6s 6d.[27] On board as host was Charles Grant, who was one of the commissioners and who had until not long before been a long-serving Member of Parliament for Inverness county; with him were landowners and others connected with the canal, the magistrates of Inverness, and the Inverness Militia Band. They set out at 11.00 a.m. from the head of Muirtown Locks to the cheers of the crowd, accompanied by the commissioners' sloop *Caledonia*. They reached Fort Augustus that evening and continued at 6.00 a.m. the following morning, now on newly opened waterway. On the way down the canal and its lochs, crowds gathered at every vantage point, the band played, guns were fired in salute from on board and on shore, and more and more of the adjoining landowners came aboard. At Loch Oich, these included MacDonnell of Glengarry with his brother: the ladies of the family stood in front of the mansion house waving their handkerchiefs. Here too the *Stirling Castle* met the second *Comet*, which had come up from the west to join her. Approaching the western end of the canal, the descent of Neptune's staircase and the locks at Corpach took three hours, so that it was 5.30 p.m. when *Stirling Castle* triumphantly steamed out onto the sea, to the cheers of the passengers and a huge crowd of spectators. Triumphant arrival at Fort William was marked by a salute fired by guns from the fort itself, by a large bonfire, and by a generous supply of free whisky for the inhabitants; then, at 7.30 p.m. Mr Grant and his guests, now numbering sixty-seven gentlemen, sat down to dinner. Alexander Easton was there, and his equivalent at the east end of the canal, James Davidson; Telford apparently was not. Dinner was followed by speeches and forty or more toasts, with Glengarry taking full part, in an evening which became ever more convivial and was supposed to end at midnight but continued long after.

On the return voyage, the following day, it had been intended again to spend the night at Fort Augustus. But when the *Stirling Castle* reached that point at about 5 p.m., the night was fine and mild, the moon bright, and the party still going on: it was decided to continue up Loch Ness. At intervals successive lairds and chieftains, as the steamboat came level with their homes, were rowed ashore in the moonlight to the farewell cheers of those still on board; and eventually *Stirling Castle* reached her destination, the swing bridge at Bught a mile or so from Inverness, at around midnight.[28]

After that, the list of vessels navigating the canal shows, *Stirling Castle* went back to working mainly between Muirtown and Fort Augustus, but at approximately weekly intervals she continued down the canal to Banavie and back.[29] This suggests she was connecting with the second *Comet*'s visits to Fort William which were at, presumably, weekly intervals; and, rather than make the time-consuming descent of Neptune's Staircase, mooring at the head of these locks with a land connection onward to Corpach basin or Fort William, wherever *Comet* might be lying.

None of these voyages was in fact a full, continuous, sea-to-sea transit of the canal. This was achieved for the first time (for any vessel, sail or steam) on 28 November 1822 when the second *Comet*, with Captain Bain in command, took passengers – presumably it was in the nature of an excursion – 'from the Western to the Eastern Sea' and back again the next day. This may have been the end of her season, for *Stirling Castle*'s visits to Banavie had ceased a week earlier and did not resume until the end of March 1823.[30] After May 1823 the canal commissioners' reports, from which this information has been extracted, become less detailed but by the following May three steamboats were trading between Glasgow and Inverness via the Crinan and Caledonian Canals:[31] the second *Comet* and the *Stirling Castle* had been joined by the *Ben Nevis*, just completed by James Lang. The canal commissioners added, to their existing regulations, new regulations for steam vessels: these gave them priority at locks, but required them, when passing other vessels on the canal, to keep to the off-side from the towing path so as not to interfere with their tracking-lines.[32]

All this encouraging progress was rudely, and tragically, interrupted on 25 October 1825 when the second *Comet* was sunk in an after-dark collision on the Clyde. And whereas the wreck of the first *Comet* had at least had the redeeming feature that those on board were able to land apparently unhurt, on the second *Comet*'s sinking some sixty-three lives were lost. She was in the final stages of a voyage from Inverness to Glasgow and approaching Kempock Point, short of Gourock, in the small hours. Outward bound was the steamboat *Ayr*. Both vessels, following the coast, needed to change course off the point and doubtless kept as close to it as their pilots considered safe. In other words they were, unknowingly, on collision course. The *Ayr* was showing a light ahead; the second *Comet*, consequent on a shortage of candles on board, was not. It is a relief to learn that Captain Bain was not in command – he appears to have transferred to the newer *Ben Nevis*.[33] Captain Duncan McInnes was in command of the second *Comet*, Captain Thomas McLelland of the *Ayr*. Men had been posted as lookouts on both vessels, and the lookout on the second *Comet* spotted the *Ayr* – but too late. The two steamboats collided at speed, more-or-less head-on.

The second *Comet* sank in a matter of minutes. About thirteen people managed to get ashore: they included the captain, and some of his crew. Most of the passengers drowned, their corpses washed ashore. Many would probably have survived had the *Ayr* attempted to save them from the water; but she did not – rather, she left the scene, Captain McLelland evidently believing she too was so badly damaged that she must make for harbour immediately. She is said to have been in a sinking condition on arrival at Greenock, but nevertheless was able to sail again the following day.[34]

McInnes and his pilot, Peter McBride, were tried a couple of months later for culpable homicide. McBride was acquitted, though admonished, and McLelland, who had given evidence, was censured by the judge. McInnes

1. A huge obelisk of red granite commemorates Henry Bell near the centre of his home town, Helensburgh. (*Author*)

ERECTED IN 1872
TO THE MEMORY OF
HENRY BELL
THE FIRST IN GREAT BRITAIN WHO WAS
SUCCESSFUL IN PRACTICALLY APPLYING STEAM
POWER FOR THE PURPOSES OF NAVIGATION

BORN IN THE COUNTY OF LINLITHGOW IN 1766
DIED AT HELENSBURGH IN 1830

2. The inscription on the obelisk at Helensburgh identifies Bell's achievement. When the obelisk was first put up, people read the inscription against a background of steamers constantly passing to and fro on the Clyde beyond. (*Author*)

3. Miller's and Symington's 1788 steamboat steams across Dalswinton Loch. The engraving is based on a sketch by the artist Alexander Nasmyth, who was present; it appeared in the autobiography of his son James Nasmyth. (*Author's collection*)

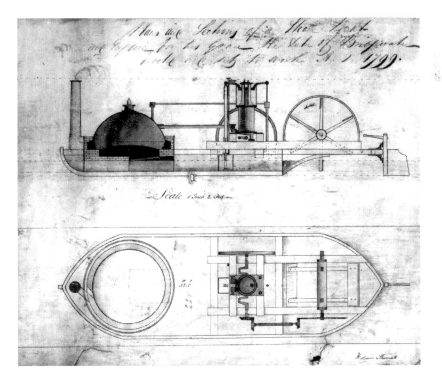

4. The forerunner of the *Charlotte Dundas*: the steamboat designed by Capt. Schank for the Duke of Bridgewater and set to work in 1799. The funnel, although it looks out of proportion, is probably shown accurately in view of the need to pass beneath canal bridges. (*The Institution of Mechanical Engineers*)

5. William Symington's second *Charlotte Dundas*, built in 1802, was demonstrated successfully on the Forth & Clyde Canal. (*J. & C. McCutcheon Collection*)

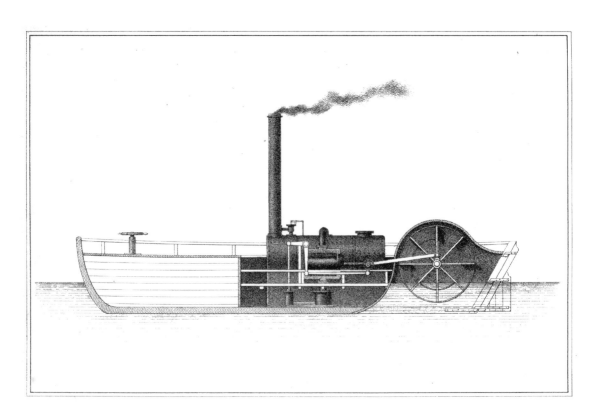

6. The layout of the steam plant in the second *Charlotte Dundas* is shown clearly in this print from Bennet Woodcroft's *Origin and Progress of Steam Navigation*. (*Author's collection*)

7. The *Clermont* steams along the Hudson River. The lithograph, which appeared in Bennet Woodcroft's *Origin and Progress of Steam Navigation*, is based on a sketch of the vessel which Woodcroft obtained from J. C. Dyer, who had travelled on her. (*Author's collection*)

TO THE GLORY OF GOD
AND IN MEMORY OF
HENRY BELL
BORN TORPHICHEN MILL 1767
DIED HELENSBURGH 1830

COMET

INVENTOR AND DESIGNER OF
EUROPES FIRST PRACTICAL STEAMSHIP
BUILT AND LAUNCHED · PORT GLASGOW
24TH JULY 1812

THIS TABLET HAS BEEN ERECTED BY
HIS GREAT GRAND NEPHEW WILLIAM BELL

8. A memorial plaque in Torphichen church commemorates Henry Bell near to his birthplace. (*Vivienne Robertson*)

9. Henry Bell's eyes twinkle as he looks out at us from a portrait by James Tannock, *c.* 1826. It would be impossible not to like such a man, even if he owed you money! (*Science and Society Picture Library*)

10. Henry Bell's distinctive Baths Inn, originally castellated, survives in Helensburgh as the central component of a later development. (*Author*)

11. John Robertson, probably about the time he built the engine which powered the *Comet*. (*Glasgow Museums*)

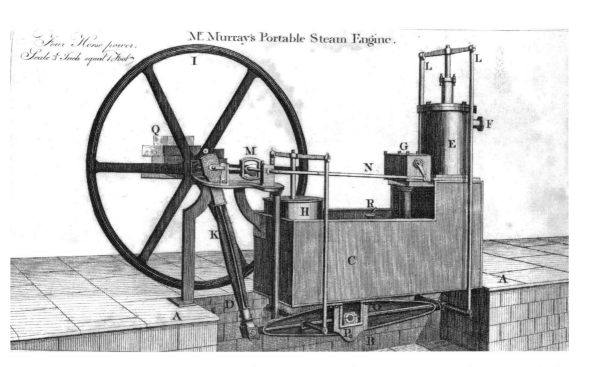

12. Layout of Matthew Murray's 'portable steam engine' of 1805 suggests it was the starting point for design of Robertson's engine for the *Comet*, and for subsequent marine steam engines. The engraving was published originally in *Nicholson's Philosophical Journal*, vol. XI. (*By permission of the Trustees of the National Library of Scotland*)

13. *Comet*'s engine is preserved in the Science Museum. Close examination shows the cylinder to be oversized for the pedestal upon which it is mounted, a reminder of the early modification which saw the original cylinder replaced by a larger one. (*Science & Society Picture Library*)

14. John Wood, when young, was the Port Glasgow shipbuilder responsible for designing and building the *Comet*. (*J. & C. McCutcheon Collection*)

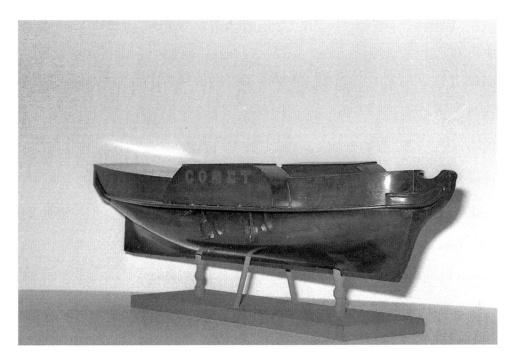

15. A builder's model of the hull of the *Comet* is displayed in the Riverside Museum, Glasgow. (*Author*)

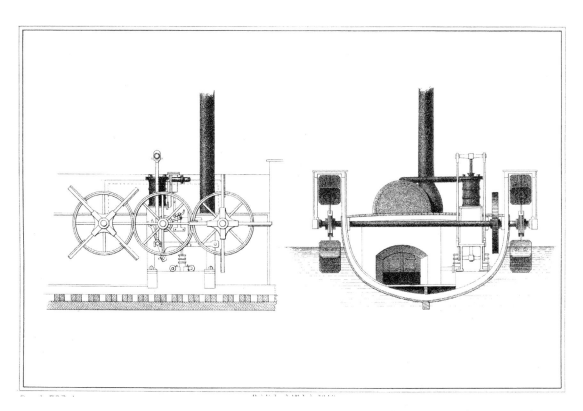

16. Layout of the machinery in *Comet*, as depicted in Woodcroft's *Origin and Progress of Steam Navigation*. It was modified many times during her career. (*Author's collection*)

17. *Comet* under way, by steam power and also taking advantage of a favourable breeze, as depicted in Woodcroft's *Origin and Progress of Steam Navigation*. Her length appears to have been exaggerated. (*Author's collection*)

18. An Arcadian scene: but the newly-commissioned *Comet* is paddling her way up the Clyde in the middle distance. Nearer at hand, a ship on the Forth & Clyde Canal can be glimpsed among the trees. (*Glasgow Museums*)

19. *Comet* at work on the Forth, in an oil painting attributed to Alexander Nasmyth. (*Science and Society Picture Library*)

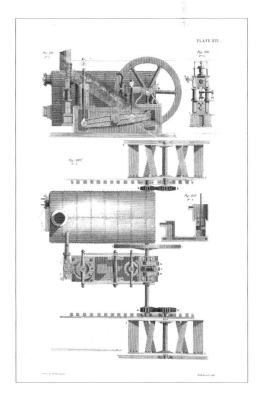

20. The machinery provided by James Cook in 1814 for the *Glasgow* and the *Argyle* is depicted in this plate from Robertson Buchanan's 1816 publication *A Practical Treatise on Propelling Vessels by Steam*. Despite poor condition, it is important: it shows clearly that these two boats were fitted with side-lever engines, possibly the earliest of their kind. (*By permission of the Trustees of the National Library of Scotland*)

21. Few early steamboats survived into the era of photography, but one that did was the *Industry* of 1814, seen here about 1870 as a hulk in Bowling Harbour. She clearly displays the bluff bows which early steamboats inherited from the design of the sailing vessels with which they were contemporary. (*Wotherspoon Collection, Mitchell Library, Glasgow*)

22. Interior of the hulk of *Industry*, *c.* 1870, with her 1828 engine still in position. It was saved and can now be seen in the Riverside Museum, Glasgow. (*Wotherspoon Collection, Mitchell Library, Glasgow*)

23. Steam and sail at the Broomielaw, Glasgow, in the 1820s, as they appeared in J. M. Leighton's *Select Views of Glasgow...* (*By permission of the Trustees of the National Library of Scotland*)

24. A steamboat, thought to be the *Glasgow*, approaches the Custom House at Greenock. (*McLean Museum & Art Gallery, Inverclyde Council*)

25. The Dorus Mór, from the heights above Craignish Point. Beyond the island, called Garbh Rèisa, a chain of islets and reefs stretches far out to sea, making this narrow passage the essential route. *Comet* came from the right, about nightfall on a December evening in 1820, rounded the point, and was forced by tide and gale onto the rocks, probably those in the foreground. (*Author*)

26. Steamboats designed and operated by B. R. Dodd on the Tyne: in the foreground is, probably, the *Eagle* of 1816, and in the right background the *Swift* of 1815. In the left background artistic licence has allowed insertion of an American steamboat, presumably for comparison. (*Science & Society Picture Library*)

27. The *Elise* arrives in Paris on 29 March 1816, prior to starting work on the Seine. She had been built on the Clyde in 1814 as the *Margery*, and had worked for a while on the Thames. (*Science & Society Picture Library*)

28. The double-hulled *Prinzessin Charlotte* was the first steamboat built in Prussia, near Spandau in 1816, and had a Boulton, Watt & Co. engine. (*Science & Society Picture Library*)

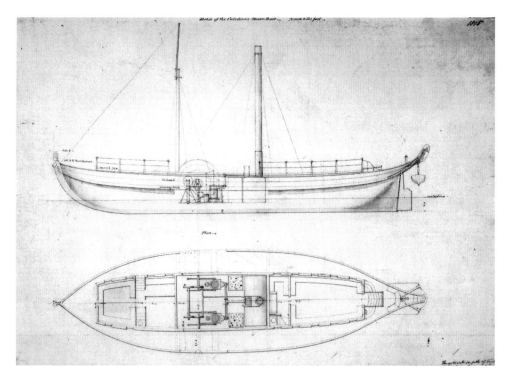

29. The *Caledonia* steamboat. Used as a floating testbed by James Watt junior in 1817–8, she crossed the North Sea to Holland and back again in the process. (*The Institution of Mechanical Engineers*)

30. 'The Queen's Visit to the Clyde, 17th August 1847', as painted by William Clark, marks the climax of the steamboat's heroic age. (*McLean Museum and Art Gallery, Inverclyde Council*)

31, 32 By day, the cabin of the Glasgow–Liverpool steamboat presented a fairly decorous scene. By the small hours, things were different. (Northern Looking Glass, c. *1825*, *Mitchell Library, Glasgow*)

33. In the early days, places at which steamboats called often lacked piers and passengers were regularly taken ashore by ferry, which had its hazards. A passenger bound for Pittenweem seems reluctant to be landed in this manner! The *Brilliant* worked between Leith and Aberdeen. (Northern Looking Glass, c. *1825*, *Mitchell Library, Glasgow*)

34. Using steam and sail, the *Enterprize* reached Calcutta in 113 days from Falmouth, arriving on 7 December 1825. She was propelled by two Maudslay, Son & Field engines with cylinders of 42-inch diameter by 48-inch stroke. (*Science and Society Picture Library*)

Above left: 35. Carved in stone, Henry Bell presides over the churchyard at Rhu, marking the grave of both himself and Margaret Bell. (*Author*)

Above right: 36. In the grass at Rhu churchyard, not far from Henry Bell's grave, is the iron gravestone which he himself provided to mark the grave of Capt. Bain, skipper of the *Comet*. (*Ann Stewart*)

37. On board the replica *Comet* at Port Glasgow in 1988 – ready to set out across a sea of motor cars! (*Author*)

38. After refurbishment in 2010–11, the replica *Comet* is again displayed in Port Glasgow, close to where both she and the original *Comet* were built. (*Author*)

was found guilty, and sentenced to three months imprisonment in Greenock jail.[35]

The public were horrified at this disaster, which was the subject of press comment and pamphlets for some time afterwards. Mariners of course were accustomed to disaster, but a head-on collision was something of which they can have had no experience in days of sail, when all vessels in the vicinity of one another were being propelled by the same breeze in more or less the same direction. It was a new risk, which came in with steamboats, and of which perhaps they had not comprehended the full seriousness. They did now. In general terms, it was a horrifying example of the fallibility of new technology.

Henry Bell, within a few days of the disaster, made a series of proposals for improving steamboat safety. Probably he circulated them to newspapers and magazines, for they were reported in detail in at least two. It seems unlikely that he was still acting as superintendent for the Comet Steamboat Company: if he was, then he acted with extreme equanimity. He did, however, as he reminded readers, write with the benefit of longer experience of steamboat operation than anyone else. He proposed legislation under which, among other things, steamboats would be licensed, their passenger numbers would be restricted according to their horsepower, their officers and engineers would be experienced men with certificates produced by the proprietors, they should carry two lights after dark, one at the bow and one at the masthead, and priorities as to the right of way for boats passing and overtaking should be established. Much of this eventually came to pass, but Bell was as ever ahead of his time.[36]

Although the second *Comet* had sunk in 17½ fathoms, the wreck was raised during the summer of 1826 and beached at Gourock. Boiler and machinery were removed, and the hull sold by auction. Despite being badly damaged by both the collision and subsequent attempts at recovery, it was repaired, rigged as a sailing vessel and saw several decades of service subsequently. The copper boiler had collapsed, because of the sudden condensation of the steam within when the boat sank, and was sold for scrap. The engine went back to its builder, D. McArthur, and was offered for sale, but the outcome is not known to the author.[37]

For Henry Bell, however, the sense of loss doubtless occasioned by the wreck of the second *Comet* must have been greatly increased by the wreck, just over two years later, of the *Stirling Castle*. In this vessel it seems he did still own a small share. She was on her way down Loch Linnhe, bound for Glasgow, on 17 January 1828 in a strong gale with showers of sleet, when the engine failed about six miles out from Fort William. She was then blown onto the rocks of Inverscaddle Bay. Most of those aboard managed to get ashore, either by boat or by jumping on to the rocks. One, sadly, was killed, and one died later that evening from injury sustained when he slipped on the rocks. It is the identity of the latter which makes this disaster particularly poignant: it was none other than MacDonnell of Glengarry, 'last of the chiefs' and sometime friend, sometime foe, to the builders of the Caledonian Canal. He and his daughters had boarded at Laggan Locks, en route for Glasgow. It seems that, while one of his daughters was being taken ashore by boat, he became concerned for her safety and, impetuous as ever, leapt from the steamboat onto a rock, slipped, and struck his head violently on a ledge.[38]

Bell, evidently, was unlucky in the fate of his steamboats. But probably he was not exceptionally so: others vessels came to similar ends. Early steamboats were prone to disaster – wrecks, sinkings, blowing up. But that was not enough to discourage people from using them, so great were their advantages – and many boats ran satisfactorily year after year. On the Caledonian Canal, which was now established as the route between Inverness and the South, more steam vessels followed and replaced those lost, although the boats in use, and their owners, changed with bewildering frequency. Notable among them was the *Maid of Morven*, built in 1826 by John Wood, with an engine by Duncan McArthur.[39] In 1836 she was involved in an incident which may have loomed larger in some peoples' minds than any physical dangers of steamboat travel. On her way from Inverness to Glasgow, she was allowed to pass through the locks at Banavie and Corpach on a Sunday; and for this the lock-keepers were summoned to appear before the kirk session of Kilmallie, for it was considered a gross violation of the Lord's day.[40] More typical no doubt was the opinion of Joseph Mitchell, who travelled the route frequently. He considered that in fine weather there was nothing more enjoyable. The mountain scenery was unequalled, and surpassed the beauties of the Rhine.[41]

Eventually the Caledonian Canal steamers became part of the MacBrayne empire, and longevity replaced the frequent changes of the early days. PS *Gondolier* became particularly well-known, for she started to carry passengers and mails between Muirtown and Banavie in 1866, and continued on this run until 1939.[42] She was the last of her line, for she was withdrawn with the outbreak of the Second World War. Subsequently, pleasure cruises (but not a scheduled end-to-end service) have been successfully re-established.[43]

While steamboat services had been spreading throughout the sheltered waters of the Scottish coastline, they had also been spreading equally rapidly elsewhere, and almost entirely as a consequence of Henry Bell's original enterprise. To these services we will now turn.

EIGHT

The Mushroom Growth of
Sheltered-Water Steamboats

When the British Association met in Glasgow in 1840, its members were
addressed by James Cleland on the trade and commerce of that city. In 1812,
he reminded them, there had been only one steam vessel in Europe, the
Comet. 'Now,' he continued, 'almost every river teems with them. It appears
… from … Parliamentary Inquiry, that on 11th February 1839, there were
766 steamers connected with the United Kingdom.'[1] By as early as 1819
about 100 steam vessels had been built in the United States; a year later,
the British Empire possessed forty-three steam boats.[2] By the end of 1823,
ninety-five steamboats had been built in Scotland, and of these forty had
been sold south of the border or abroad.[3] While the quantity and tonnage
of steamboats built in the USA continued to exceed those built in the UK,
those built in the USA were mostly for use on the long, broad rivers of that
country where, throughout much of it, roads were few and the forests that
lined the banks provided a limitless source of fuel. In Europe, on the other
hand, land communications were already good, coal (bulky but not so bulky
as wood) was the fuel, and the UK in particular had an incentive to develop
steamers suitable for open water.[4]

Nevertheless, the first great blossoming of steamboat services in the Old
World took place on the sheltered estuaries and coastal waters of the UK,
and before long on the rivers and estuaries of Europe. Short sea routes
followed, and steam power was, after some initial hesitation, adopted with
enthusiasm by the Royal Navy. Eventually, and more slowly, ocean-going
steamers were developed.

Steamboats – the mechanism

All this needed, and in turn encouraged, technical developments in the steam plant used, although for a couple of decades the side lever engine remained the conventional type of engine – often two side lever engines were installed as a pair. The Trevithick-type high pressure engine was an early but eventually unsuccessful rival. Other types of low-pressure engine were tried. The oscillating engine, a compact layout introduced in the 1820s, had cylinders which oscillated so that the centre line of the cylinder remained in line with the crankpin: this made possible direct drive, with piston rod coupled direct to crank.[5] Marc Isambard Brunel patented in 1822 the 'Triangle Engine', for marine or land use, in which the cylinders were laid out as an inverted V, with direct drive to the crankshaft.[6] David Napier introduced the 'steeple engine' about 1831: the cylinder was positioned vertically just below the crankshaft, with piston rods, two or four of them, passing upwards either side of the shaft to an elevated crosshead, from which the connecting rod descended to the crankshaft – an arrangement which minimised the floor space the engine occupied.[7] None of these initially made much impact on use of the side-lever engine, although all did later on.

The boilers of early steamboats were large, rectangular boxes, made of wrought iron, or copper. Within them were rectangular furnaces, and from these the flues – flat-sided passageways – wound maze-like between the water spaces to reach, eventually, the base of the funnel. The water spaces were a few inches wide, the flues wide enough for men to enter them regularly to scrape off accumulated soot. To dislodge soot from the funnel, a musket might be fired up it. The fires had to be extinguished every few days in any case: since boilers were fed with salt water, it was at first the practice to empty them at this interval to prevent excessive concentrations of salt. Later on they were blown down – that is to say, steam and water were discharged in limited amounts – every few hours instead. In principle the answer to this problem should have been the surface condenser, in which exhaust steam would be condensed by passing it through pipes immersed in cold water, so that pure condensate could be fed back into the boiler. But although there were attempts to do so in the 1820s and 1830s, making a satisfactory surface condenser seems to have been beyond the technical capacity of the period, and it was several decades more before such equipment became usual.[8]

Steam pressures were, by later standards, very low – only a few pounds per square inch. Weighted safety valves were fitted. With a gradual increase in steam pressures, up to around 20 lb per sq. in, multi-tubular boilers started to enter marine practice in the late 1830s and early 1840s.[9]

After boiler and engine, the other conspicuously vital component of a paddle steamer is the paddle wheels themselves. On the earliest steamboats, the paddles or floats were fixed to radial arms. Clearly each paddle was at its most efficient only when vertical in the water or nearly so, and very much less efficient when entering or leaving the water. This was a problem which occupied the minds of many ingenious men, but a satisfactory feathering paddle wheel, which maintained the floats at the most advantageous angle to the water, taking into account the passage of the boat through it, had appeared by the end of the 1820s.[10]

Over the paddle wheels, each side, were the paddle boxes; and since these often projected high above the deck, the tops of the paddle boxes became convenient if exposed positions where the captain might stand to oversee navigation of the boat and give orders to his crew. In due course an elevated 'bridge' was provided between the tops of the two paddle boxes, and on this the captain, and in due course the helmsman, took up their positions.

Estuary Steamboats – the East Coast of England

In 1818, only six years after Henry Bell's pioneering venture on the Clyde, George Dodd (whose adventurous voyage from the Clyde to the Thames was described in chapter five) listed the following locations at which steamboats were at work in the British Isles: Clyde, Tay, Trent, Tyne, Humber, Mersey, Yare, Avon, Severn, Orwell, Forth, Cork, and Thames.[11]

Of these, the first in the field outside Scotland was the River Yare, in Norfolk. As early as 1811 or possibly 1812, John Wright, a Norwich Quaker, bought a captured French privateer, a 52-foot open boat powered by three lugsails and twenty oars. He and his brother Richard then spent a lot of time and money attempting to install a primeval internal combustion engine powered by hydrogen. When this proved a failure, it was removed and the boat sailed to the Humber and taken up the Aire & Calder Navigation to Leeds, there to have a steam engine installed by Fenton, Murray & Wood. When he had publicised his portable engine in 1805, Matthew Murray had noted the possibility of working it with high pressure steam, non-condensing, although he was hesitant about adopting this practice at the time. In 1812 he did so, however, in the locomotives he built for the Middleton Railway, the layout of which was based on Trevithick's ideas. In 1813 he followed this by building a Trevithick-type high pressure engine and installing it in Wright's boat. Probably the engine followed Trevithick's usual pattern, with a cylindrical boiler containing a cylindrical flue of large diameter for the fire, and with the cylinder recessed into the boiler also. Its 'high pressure' was probably as much as 30 lb per sq. in.[12]

The work was complete enough by 18 June 1813 for the new steamboat to run trials on the River Aire. This attracted a great concourse of spectators to the banks, according to the local paper, who saw the boat go down the river and up again with astonishing velocity. By the end of July she was at Hull, on her way south.[13]

She had been insured for the sea voyage on condition that the paddle wheels were unshipped and the engine not worked: she was to go by sail alone. Soon after leaving the Humber, however, an easterly gale sprung up and drove her ashore, where she became beached when the tide receded. Richard Wright, who was on board, then had her propped up. Insurance conditions or no, he re-installed the paddle wheels and raised steam: as soon as she floated with the return of the tide, he steamed her out to sea. Once well off-shore he probably started sailing again, and stopped using the engine. Like this he safely reached Yarmouth.[14]

The *Experiment*, as the boat had been re-named (her original name appears to have been *L'Actif*) ran a private excursion on 9 August 1813 and then went into service the following day between Yarmouth and Norwich. Evidently she was a success, for John Wright had a second steamboat built about 1814, also with a high pressure engine, and called the *Telegraph*. Subsequently a new hull was built and the engine from *Experiment* transferred to it – this new vessel was the *Courier*. Other steamboats were built for other local owners.

At one stage the *Telegraph* was steamed down to the Medway to work between Sheerness and Chatham. The Medway's currents proved too much for her, however, and after a couple of months she returned to Norfolk. It was then found that as a consequence of the sea voyage her boiler had become badly encrusted with saline deposits, and during the course of repairs a new cast-iron end plate was bolted on to a boiler otherwise of wrought iron.[15] This course of action would, unfortunately, prove to be the root cause of disaster.

On Good Friday, 4 April, 1817 the *Telegraph* was preparing to depart from Norwich. So was a competing steamboat, the *Nelson*. The *Telegraph* was ready first but, just after she had left her mooring, the boiler exploded. Some fragments burst through the fore-cabin, others through the aft cabin. Nine people were killed and six seriously injured, of whom two later died. Others had lucky escapes: the steward, on deck, was blown into the air but came down again to land unhurt where the boiler had been, and a baby in a cradle under a seat also escaped unharmed. The engineer, severely scalded, was blown into the river but was able to swim to the bank. He was thought, although he denied it, to have weighted the safety valve down to obtain the speed needed to defeat the competition; the cast iron end to the boiler had given way.[16]

To the present author, the surprising thing is that the boiler should have burst just when it did. The immediate effect of setting the engine in motion by drawing steam from the boiler must have been to reduce the boiler pressure. Maybe it was on the on the point of going anyway and vibration from the machinery, mounted upon the boiler, was the last straw.

Several noted engineers, George Dodd among them, soon assembled at Norwich with a view to gathering information about the cause of the disaster and its effects, and to suggest means to prevent similar accidents. But they could not agree. Dodd says he then suggested to friends in the House of Commons that the subject was fit for Parliamentary investigation. The outcome was the Select Committee to consider 'the means of preventing the mischief of Explosion from happening on board STEAM-BOATS, to the danger or destruction of His Majesty's Subjects…'. The committee started to sit on 13 May 1817 and made its report, with commendable promptitude, on 24 June. (The speed with which, two centuries ago, such things could be organised, compared with our own supposedly more advanced times, is always an eye-opener!) Those who gave evidence to it included Bryan Donkin; George Dodd; Andrew Vivian, an associate of Trevithick (who was then in Peru); and Richard Wright himself, who stated that steamboat enginemen were in the habit of loading safety valves and he believed the steam pressure before the explosion to have been more than 75 lb per sq. in. in a boiler intended for 40 lb. Another who gave evidence was Seth Hunt, an American who pointed out that although some of the many American steamboats had high pressure boilers, none had boilers of cast iron and all which passed through salt water had boilers of copper.[17]

The Select Committee in its report expressed the view that while the legislature should avoid interfering in private concerns or property, and particularly in the exercise of mechanical ingenuity, yet there were circumstances in which it must do so in the interest of the safety of the public. Its proposals included: all steamboat boilers to be of wrought iron or copper; boilers to be inspected and their strength certified prior to use; boilers to have two safety valves, one of them inaccessible to the engineman; safety valves to be inspected and certified to open at one third of the pressure to which the boiler had been proved; a penalty to be placed on anyone putting an extra weight on the safety valves. The immediate legislation upon which the committee resolved does not seem to have happened – but most of these measures, or something like them, did eventually become standard practice.[18]

The high-pressure engine had offered, by comparison with the low-pressure condensing engine, compactness, lightness and simplicity of construction. But the evident risk of disaster from explosion was enough to halt its development, at this period, for marine use. Engines derived from those of Trevithick would, within a decade or two, see rapid development for land use, on rails; but on the water, engines derived from the Watt condensing engine would continue to be usual, pressures only being increased gradually until much later in the eighteenth century. There had been earlier boiler explosions, and there were more to come, but none so devastating, particularly in effect on public opinion, as that of 1817.

Writing to Simon Goodrich in 1815, Matthew Murray said of the steamboat working between Hull and Gainsborough that it 'was made in Scotland and is but a very indifferent thing.'[19] The boat was Robertson's *Caledonia*, and since Robertson was a good engineer, Murray's strange comment needs to be read in the knowledge that it is being applied to a boat with a low-pressure engine by one who was already supplying high-pressure machinery for boats – but that the disadvantages of this had still to make themselves dramatically apparent. Robertson himself, probably a better engineer than businessman, seems to have been unable to make his Humber steamboats pay, and sold out after about eighteen months.[20] Others were more successful and by 1819 *Caledonia* was working between Selby and Hull, carrying passengers brought by coach from Leeds and Wakefield, and parcels brought by waggon from as far afield as Manchester. Competing steamboats were appearing, and steamboat services had been extended – in 1816 up the Ouse to York and up the Don to Thorne, and in 1817 as far up the Trent as Nottingham.[21]

'Mr Dodd,' wrote Henry Creighton to his brother in 1813, 'is puffing away at Newcastle and going to go 8 miles an hour to Shields.'[22] The 'Mr Dodd' to whom he referred was Barrodall Robert Dodd, elder brother of George. From Creighton's comment it sounds as though he was planning to use a high-pressure engine, the characteristic of which was that they puffed – or perhaps he just had a bombastic manner. The vessel concerned was launched at Gateshead in February 1814 and known as the *Tyne Steamboat* or *Tyne Steam Packet*: she went into service carrying passengers between Newcastle and Shields. In 1817 she was sold to a local businessman, Joseph Price, who renamed her *Perseverance* and used her as a tug to tow sailing ships up and down the river and out to sea – the first of a long line of steam paddle tugs on the Tyne.[23]

By then there appear to have been two other steamboats at work on the Tyne, both of them built under B. R. Dodd's direction: the *Swift* of 1815, and the *Eagle* of 1816 for which Boulton, Watt Co. provided the engine. Henry Creighton conducted some trials with this boat soon after she was launched, but an application to run further trials the following year was refused. 'The experiments would take a week,' Creighton wrote to his brother, 'Tyne Co. blackguards and scoundrels as they are, were in the right to grumble at [Boulton, Watt & Co.'s] using the boat for experiments, and with sufficient cause too.'[24]

While Wright's *Experiment* was showing what a steamboat could do on the Yare in 1813, another steamboat was being built at Great Yarmouth. The builder was James Lepingwell, and a local foundry supplied the engine. But this proved insufficiently powerful, and a replacement was obtained from the noted London engineers H. Maudslay & Co., to whom reference is made below; it was delivered by sea. Thus equipped, the *Orwell* went into service on the river of its name, between Ipswich and Harwich, in 1815. But this service was not a success, and lasted apparently for only a few weeks, after which, strangely, the *Orwell* seems to disappear from history.[25]

The Thames, Tideway and Estuary

The Thames would come, for a few decades, to occupy as important a place as the Clyde in encouraging the rapid spread of passenger travel by steamboats, and in due course the more general use of steamships of ever-increasing dimensions. One of the most influential persons in this process, perhaps the most influential, was Henry Maudslay – pioneer of accuracy in engineering and pioneer of accurate machine tools, who had made his name as the constructor of machinery, to Marc Isambard Brunel's designs, to mass produce pulley-blocks for the sailing ships of the Royal Navy. This machinery, the first instance of mass production, was installed at Portsmouth Dockyard during 1802–1809. Maudslay became part of a close-knit group of influential persons including Marc Isambard Brunel, Samuel Bentham, Simon Goodrich and Maudslay's junior partner, Joshua Field. It was almost inevitable that, when his works started to manufacture marine steam engines, he would become one of the most noted manufacturers.[26]

In view of this, it is surprising that there is doubt over the identity of the vessel for which he first built an engine, and indeed doubt over the identity of the first steamboat to enter service on the Thames. It is clear that Maudslay built the engine for the steamboat *Richmond*, which was built at Great Yarmouth and went into service between London, Richmond and Twickenham in, probably, 1815,[27] or perhaps 1814.[28] Either then or soon afterwards, she came under George Dodd's supervision.[29] It is also said that the engine for this vessel was Maudslay's first marine engine, and was built in 1815.[30] This appears potentially to conflict with the *Orwell*, mentioned above. It seems quite possible that the *Orwell*, which as mentioned above ran for a few weeks in 1815 on the river of its name and then disappeared, was renamed to become the *Richmond*. But the evidence is solely circumstantial, and no confirmation has come to the author's attention. On the other hand, the chronological list of steamboats included as an appendix to the 1822 report of the Select Committee on Holyhead Roads lists both *Orwell* and *Richmond* separately. It states that both were built by Lepingwell and equipped with machinery respectively by Agg & Ker of Norwich and by Maudslay; *Orwell* it dates to as early as 1813, and *Richmond* to 1814.[31] This list was prepared by Joshua Field, and although it does contain some evident errors, in this instance he may be expected have got it right. It is quite likely though that Maudslay's engine was ordered in 1814 and, if so, Field may been aware of this and that it was shipped to Lepingwell at Great Yarmouth, and in due course reappeared in London fitted into a steamboat called *Richmond*, while he failed to make the connection with *Orwell*. It is all yet another instance of the uncertainties surrounding the history of early steamboats.

The *Richmond* was joined on her up-river route in 1817 by the *London*, built under Dodd's direction; to pass under low bridges, both were fitted with lowering funnels, invented by Dodd.[32] Lowering the funnel to pass beneath a bridge became a practice which was to remain familiar on river steamers until recent times. In 1817, 10,000 passengers travelled on these two boats within four months.[33] Other vessels in due course joined them.

Important though the up-river route from London was, that which went down-river was far more so. The principal goals were Gravesend, Margate and, later on, Southend. Gravesend in the second decade of the nineteenth century was a popular resort, Margate a fashionable one. As on the Clyde, salt water bathing was the great attraction. The journey from London to Margate by sailing vessel – a 'hoy' as they were called – took between ten hours and three days, according to the weather. The alternative was 15 hours in a stagecoach.[34] This was the market for which *Margery* and *Thames* were brought south.

The *Margery* reached London in time to make her first trip, between Wapping and Gravesend, on 23 January 1815. She was probably the first steamboat to go into service on the Thames tideway, although *Richmond* may have preceded her. She then operated on this route for several months, but regrettably she does not seem to have been particularly reliable. She had frequently to be withdrawn for repairs, which sometimes took as long as ten days, and the longest period for which she was in service continuously was three weeks. At the end of the season she was withdrawn, but she was then re-fitted and sold, or chartered, in 1816 for service in France on the River Seine, as will be mentioned below.[35]

So the true progenitor of successful steamboat services on the Thames estuary became George Dodd's steamboat *Thames*. She went into service between London and Margate on 3 July 1815.[36] A couple of years later, Dodd told the Select Committee on explosions on steamboats that she had been in service on the Thames for two years, laid up in winter, and that he had just obtained a new boiler for her from Butterley. By then he had five steamboats under his direction: two to Richmond, one to Gravesend and two to Margate.[37] The Margate boats covered the distance of 88 miles by water in 11 hours on average, occasionally in as little as 8 hours. Sometimes there was a band on board, and dancing.[38] The second of Dodd's Margate steamboats was the *Majestic*. This vessel, built at Ramsgate in 1816, had come under his supervision when the owners applied to him to remedy defects in her design and construction, which he appears to have done to their satisfaction. Both she and the *Thames* were often also used to tow sailing ships down-river when contrary winds prevented their sailing.[39]

By then, others had entered the field. One of them was Marc Isambard Brunel. Some sources suggest he was experimenting as early as 1814 or even earlier, which may or may not be correct. However, a steamboat to his design was built at Rotherhithe – the first steam vessel built on the Thames. Maudslay provided the engines, and the vessel is recorded as being fitted out during August 1815. Initially she was equipped with a single 8-foot-wide paddle wheel central within the hull, but although the layout provided for water to reach the wheel and to be driven away from it, the arrangements proved inadequate; the central paddle wheel was removed and the usual pair of external paddle wheels provided. The boiler was on the centre line of the hull and there were two engines, one each side of it. Thus equipped, the *Regent*, as this boat was called, went into service between London and Margate in 1816, apparently with great success. Not that this immediately pleased everyone – particularly those with an interest in the sailing vessels between London and Margate: Brunel himself later recalled having been refused a bed in a Margate hotel because he had arrived by steamboat.[40]

Unfortunately, on 2 July 1817, when off Whitstable, the *Regent* caught fire – probably because part of the deck had been built too close to the funnel, the heat from which ignited the dry wood. The fire proved impossible to extinguish and drove the men from the engine room: the captain then steered for Whitstable beach, the engines going faster and faster (the fire around the boiler caused steam pressure to rise, presumably). There he ran her aground, losing his ship but saving the lives of all on board.[41]

Other early Thames steamboats included the *Sons of Commerce*, built in 1817 with a Butterley engine for the Gravesend route, which nevertheless proved a good sea-going vessel and fast, so that she was transferred to the Margate run in place of the *Regent*.[42] The *Britannia* started a service between London and Southend the same year.[43] The very large – 120 feet long – *London Engineer* built in 1818 for the Margate route was provided with engines by Maudslay, Sons & Field: with her, Maudslay made another attempt to use paddle wheels placed inboard. They were either side of the keel, in an airtight compartment. Because the paddle shaft was only about 15 inches above the water level, compressed air was introduced into the airtight compartment to lower the water level within it – an arrangement patented ten years earlier by Richard Trevithick and an associate. Presumably the intention was to lower the centre of gravity of the vessel, and so minimise any tendency to roll. But despite high hopes, she does not seem to have been particularly successful.[44]

By then, steamboats were appearing thick and fast on the Thames. According to Sherwood, in 1820 there were nine steamboats operating from London; ten years later there were fifty-seven.[45] The General Steam Navigation Company, established in 1825, became a prominent operator:[46] since it was also much concerned with short sea routes, there is more about it below. The increase in numbers was not achieved without incident and accident, and in 1825 the City Corporation found it necessary to make safety regulations concerning the speed of steamboats; subsequently regulations were enhanced and tightened up on several occasions without, it seems, becoming particularly effective.[47]

This first period of steamboat prosperity came to it its end with construction of the railway system, even though the intended function of the London & Blackwall Railway of 1840 was to provide, in a manner comparable to the Glasgow, Paisley & Greenock Railway, an accelerated link with estuary steamboats by cutting out the up-river part of their voyages. On the Thames Estuary, however, unlike the Firth of Clyde, there were no geographical features to prevent railway construction along one of the shores, and the importance of the estuary steamer as a means of transport was soon much reduced. Regular sailings by pleasure steamer, however, continued to be a familiar feature of the Thames estuary well into the latter half of the twentieth century.[48]

Estuaries and Canals – the South and the West

In the South, the Chichester and Arundel Canal, part of the inland route between Portsmouth and London which was not exposed to French attack, built itself a steam tug in 1820. This, the *Earl of Egremont*, was engined by Maudslay.[49] The first steamboat to operate between Southampton and Cowes was the *Prince of Coburg*, built on the Trent at Gainsborough in 1817 and transferred to the South Coast in 1820. A second vessel, the *Medina*, was added in 1822, and two more in 1826.[50]

A steamboat was built for the Bristol Avon as early as 1813, to ply between Bristol and Bath. The owner was Theodore Lawrence, and the vessel, called *Hope*, was a small one, about 50 feet long. Lawrence took his boat through the canal system to the Thames and attempted to operate her there, but opposition from the Watermen's Company was too strong – so he took her back to the Avon and resumed operation on that river. Several early sources mention Lawrence and his steamboat,[51] but none known to the author offers any insight into how this venture came about. So it is interesting to note that the portrait of John Robertson which hangs in the Riverside Museum was attributed, according to the painted inscription on the frame, to 'T. Lawrence', and one may speculate on the possibility of a link.

On the River Severn, a steamboat to carry passengers and luggage went into service between Worcester and Gloucester in 1814. Towing by steam tug was eventually introduced in 1830.[52]

In Ireland, the steamboat *City of Cork*, powered by Boulton, Watt & Co. engines, went into service between Cork and Cove (now Cobh) in 1815.[53] Local steamer services from Cork then operated continuously for the next 110 years, and excursions continued subsequently.[54] On the Grand Canal, one of the directors, James Dawson, had been experimenting with steam power, probably since as early as 1811, and in 1813 demonstrated the resulting vessel to his co-directors. This steamboat too was named *Comet*, presumably after the same phenomenon that had attracted Henry Bell's attention. It had two keels with the paddle wheel mounted between them, to enable it to pass through the canal's locks, which would take boats of no more than 13-foot, 7½-inch beam. Although it appears to have performed satisfactorily during trials, it did not go into service, but Dawson is said to have put a steamboat into operation between London and Gravesend in 1818.[55] On the many inland loughs in Ireland the first steamer appeared in 1821 on Lough Neagh, in the form of the *Marchioness of Donegall*. This was built by the Lagan Navigation Co., with engines by David Napier, to tow its canal boats across the lough.[56]

Back across the Irish Sea, when the *Elizabeth* reached the Mersey from the Clyde she was put into service between Liverpool and Runcorn. This was an old-established route for sailing packets: from Runcorn there were connections onward to Manchester by horse-drawn packet boats on both the Mersey & Irwell Navigation and the rival Duke of Bridgewater's Canal. But although *Elizabeth* had operated successfully on the Clyde, this success does not seem to have been repeated on the Mersey. In 1816 she was sold again and converted into a horse-drawn packet boat. But she had evidently shown what could be done; by then, other steamboats were building for the route, they went into service in 1817 and steam packets then became a lasting feature of it.[57] Steam ferry services across, rather than along, the Mersey started in 1816, and in the same year steamboats were first used to tow sailing ships out to sea from Liverpool.[58] Steamboat services on the Dee, going downstream from Chester, started in 1817.[59]

On the Continent

While steamboat services were springing up on the rivers and estuaries of the British Isles, they were also starting to appear on the Continent, and usually there was a connection with what was happening in Britain. One of the first steamboats to be built on the Continent for service there was another *Elizabeth*, for which there was a direct link to the work of the Scottish pioneers. She was built in 1815 at St Petersburg for service on the River Neva, and was the brainchild of Charles Baird. As a young man in 1786, Baird had been one of a dozen skilled workmen lured away from Carron Ironworks to Russia, initially to erect blast furnace equipment which Carron was sending out. Baird prospered and by 1815 was a partner in one of the largest engineering works in Russia.

Charles Baird's father was Nicol Baird, superintendent of the Forth & Clyde Canal, and one of his brothers was Hugh Baird, who eventually succeeded their father and became a noted engineer in his own right. Charles Baird kept in touch with his family at home, and is said to have followed assiduously the latest British engineering developments. He was well-placed to be fully aware of the emerging development of the steamboat through the work of Symington and Bell. Fulton too had been making overtures to the Russian authorities since as early as 1811, with a view to introducing steamboats there, and it can be conjectured that Baird was aware of this. At any rate, it is no surprise to find that in 1815 he was rebuilding a wooden barge and equipping it with side-lever engine and paddle wheels which even at this early date had feathering floats. This was the *Elizabeth*. She went into service between St Petersburg and Kronstadt; an early visitor on board was the dowager Empress. Two years later Baird built a second steamboat for the route, the layout of which vessel is said to have resembled closely that of Bell's *Comet*.[60]

The *Margery*, re-fitted for service in France and re-named *Elise*, became the first steam vessel to cross the Channel when she made a seventeen-hour crossing against head winds from Newhaven to Rouen in March 1816. Those on board included Captain Pierre Andriel of her new operator, Andriel, Pajol et Cie. Also present were Anthony Cortis, and W. Jackson, who had earlier been an associate of Fulton. *Elise* ascended the River Seine to make a triumphant arrival in Paris at the end of the month, and then descended the river again to start a service between Rouen and Elbeuf.[61]

A sea-crossing which was if anything even more ambitious was made the same year by the Stirling Steamboat Company's *Lady of the Lake*. She crossed the North Sea to Hamburg, and then during 1817–18 plied on the Elbe between Hamburg and Cuxhaven. This was evidently in the nature of a charter, for late in 1818 she crossed back to Leith and then resumed her former station between Leith and Stirling.[62] One suspects that it is no coincidence that 1816 to 1818 were also the years when Henry Bell, having fallen out with the Stirling company, was operating both *Stirling* and *Comet* on the Forth, before removing them to the Caledonian Canal and the west coast.

Meanwhile, the first steamboat to be built in Prussia was launched near Berlin in September 1816. She was the *Prinzessin Charlotte*, a double-hulled vessel with the deck extending over both hulls and a central paddle wheel driven by a side-lever engine supplied by Boulton, Watt & Co. She went into use on the rivers Elbe, Havel and Spree. The following year Boulton, Watt & Co. supplied the machinery for the steamer *Die Weser*, built near Bremen for service, presumably, on the river of its name, and subsequently they supplied the machinery for more steamers for the service pioneered by *Prinzessin Charlotte*.[63]

The first steamboats in Sweden were the work of Samuel Owen, who is known as the 'Founder of Swedish Mechanical Industry'. Owen served his apprenticeship with Boulton & Watt, and later moved to Fenton Murray

& Wood. It seems that he first went to Sweden in 1804 on their behalf, but by 1809 he had settled there and opened his own engineering works in Stockholm. In 1816 he produced an experimental steam boat, the *Waterwitch*, and followed this two years later with the *Amphitrite*, which went into commercial service on Lake Mälaren.[64]

One of the most remarkable episodes in the spread of British steamboat technology is that of the steamboat *Caledonia*, built on the Clyde in 1815. By 1816 she was on the Thames at London, and in 1817 she was bought by Boulton, Watt & Co. It appears that Henry Bell acted as agent. James Watt jun. was in charge of the marine engine side of Boulton, Watt & Co.'s business. Many engine builders were based in ports so steamboats, their layout and behaviour in operation, had become a familiar part of daily life. For Boulton, Watt & Co., based in the English Midlands, this experience was lacking. With their own vessel (even though it seemed to some that Watt was using her as a pleasure yacht) they could catch up on this lack of practical experience, and carry out tests and trials in their own time on engine, boat and paddle wheels.[65]

Caledonia was fitted with a pair of new 14 hp engines of Boulton, Watt & Co.'s own manufacture, and Watt jun. himself then carried out trials with *Caledonia*, possibly in association with John Rennie, and concentrating on speed and coal consumption. The location was the Thames estuary, and on occasion *Caledonia* went down as far as Margate. The trials were in public and there were opportunist tests of speed against the *Thames* and the *Sons of Commerce*, to both of which *Caledonia* showed herself superior.[66]

That autumn it was decided to test her capabilities further by taking her across the North Sea to Rotterdam and back, under command of Capt. Wager RN, who had made a cross-channel journey by steam the previous year. Watt jun., aware of his father's likely reaction to such a venture, apparently kept quiet about it until after safe arrival in Rotterdam! Indeed overall the voyage was not without incident. At one point the pilot, whose knowledge of the Dutch coast had been gained in a previous career as a smuggler, managed to run *Caledonia* aground. It took the entire population of a nearby village, plus four horses, to pull her free. Elsewhere one of the engine beams broke; this meant having a replica cast at a foundry, and then fitting it, which with Watt jun. hard at work with the rest of his crew was achieved within four days. But on return it was considered that otherwise the machinery had acted perfectly well throughout, and the vessel had ridden the waves extremely well also. To Watt the practicability of using steam vessels for short sea passages was confirmed.[67]

Further experiments were carried out with *Caledonia* during 1818, but eventually James Watt jun. found it necessary to 'part with her with regret',[68] selling her to Danish owners who took her back across the North Sea to Copenhagen. She continued to ply in that area until the early 1840s.[69] Meanwhile Boulton, Watt & Co., having initially failed to capitalise on their early pioneering manufacture of steamboat engines for Fulton, had by 1822 built more marine steam engines for use in the British Isles than any other manufacturer.[70]

NINE

The Seagoing Steamer Appears

Following the successful introduction of steamboats to the Firth of Clyde, two steamboats, the *Britannia* and the *Hibernia*, were built to the order of Dublin owners for service between Dublin and Holyhead, with the intention that they should eventually carry the mails. They were built by James Munn of Greenock, with engines by James Cook, which could have been enough to secure success, and when they first went into service in 1816 they did at first appear successful.[1] But they were soon perceived as failures, possibly because their design was too closely based on that of Clyde steamboats, and neither the form of their hulls, nor the strength of their hulls, engine, paddles and rigging was adequate for the much rougher conditions regularly encountered in the Irish Sea.[2]

After this false start it was left to David Napier to build the first successful steamer intended for service on the open sea. First he took passage on one of the sailing packets between Glasgow and Belfast, stationing himself in the bow, regardless of a storm, to observe the effects of the waves on the ship when they were at their fiercest. He followed this with experiments on model hulls upon a mill-dam, and deduced that a much finer bow was needed than the bluff bows which existing steamboats had inherited from sailing vessels.[3] The result was the *Rob Roy*, built for Napier in 1818 by William Denny at Dumbarton, 75 feet long with a single 32 hp side-lever engine. Napier put her into service between Glasgow and Belfast, over which route she reliably carried passengers and mails for the next two years. He followed this with the *Talbot* (1819) and the *Ivanhoe* (1820), which successfully went into service on the Holyhead–Howth route.[4]

Another open-water steamer service, between Liverpool and Dublin, also started at this time.[5]

The steamer service between Glasgow and Liverpool started in 1819, the first vessel being the *Robert Bruce*, with a Napier engine. For many years this route offered a popular and competitive alternative to coach travel between the two cities.[6] It was through travelling over this route in 1826 in the steamer *Henry Bell* that Bell's biographer Edward Morris first became aware of Bell and his story,[7] as described in chapter ten.

On the east coast, steamers started to ply between Leith and London in 1821. Sir Walter Scott, going south for the coronation of George IV, was a passenger on one of them, the *City of Edinburgh*. It should, he felt, have been better called *The New Reekie* – but the advantage was clear of a new means of transport which took 60 hours and cost 3 guineas, compared with a post-chaise in 7 days at a cost of £30–40.[8] The mail coach would have been quicker than a post-chaise, but less comfortable. Another steamer which entered service on the same route at this time was the *James Watt*, built by Wood & Co. with a Boulton, Watt & Co. engine for a London syndicate headed by Thomas Brocklebank. Brocklebank was a Deptford timber merchant who already owned the Margate steamer *Eagle*.[9] A later vessel for the same route was the *United Kingdom* of 1826, built by Robert Steele & Co. at Greenock and engined by David Napier. Possibly the largest steam vessel of her day, she was too large to pass through the Caledonian Canal and in order to reach Leith had to voyage by the Mull of Kintyre, Stornoway, Stromness and Peterhead – her proprietors turned this to their advantage by making it a luxury cruise and attracting some 120 passengers. Once at work, she reduced the time for the voyage from London to Leith to 40–50 hours.[10] Steamer services between the east coast ports soon became widespread.

After two years on the Irish Sea, Napier's *Rob Roy* was moved to the South in 1821 to work between Dover and Calais – the first cross-Channel steamer service.[11] The next decade saw the appearance of many other steamship routes between England and the Continent, short routes such as London–Calais, Dover–Boulogne, Brighton–Dieppe, and longer ones such as London–Rotterdam and London–Hamburg. Much of this was a result of the enterprise of the General Steam Navigation Co., which evolved out of Brocklebank's syndicate and became a familiar feature of east coast shipping services until the 1960s.[12]

The Royal Navy

After Stanhope's experiments, the Navy's introduction to the practicalities of steam power came in 1799 when Samuel Bentham had a 12 hp pumping engine installed at Portsmouth,[13] and followed this with the pioneering steam dredgers described in chapter two.

Henry Bell, late in life, made graphic claims to have drawn the attention of the Admiralty to the value of steam propulsion as early as 1800, and again in 1803, without success.[14] Brian Osborne has comprehensively demolished these claims in his biography *The Ingenious Mr Bell*.[15] And yet, the naval authorities were certainly in touch with both Fulton[16] and Trevithick[17] at that period or soon after. As ever, even with Bell's most preposterous claims, one is left wondering whether deep within them there may not be some tiny kernel of fact. Osborne, however, convincingly suggests that Bell had considered the approach he did indeed make to the Admiralty in 1813 and, in his enthusiasm for establishing priority over other steamboat pioneers, transferred it in his mind to a period a decade earlier.[18]

Bell's 1813 proposals were among many such which the Admiralty was receiving at this period, and the response was discouraging.[19] Matthew Murray seems to have had no better luck when he approached Simon Goodrich on the subject in 1815.[20] The hesitancy displayed by naval authority to steam power at this period seems to have been a consequence of more than simple conservatism. Britannia had successfully ruled the waves during the Napoleonic wars from which she was just emerging by use of traditional methods. Any introduction of new technologies at sea seemed as likely to reduce that superiority as enhance it.[21] Nor can matters have been helped by the dual nature of naval administration at this period, with the Navy Board, which was responsible for supply, operating in tandem with the Board of Admiralty. They did not see eye to eye. The two would eventually amalgamate in 1832.

In 1815, however, a proposal was made to the Admiralty for use of steam propulsion, in specialised circumstances, from a source so distinguished that it could scarcely be ignored. This was Sir Joseph Banks, who had accompanied Captain James Cook around the world between 1768 and 1771, and had been President of the Royal Society continuously since 1778. He had also, among much else, been appointed in 1804 to the British Government commission set up to examine Fulton's torpedo proposals, and to supervise experiments. John Rennie was another of the commissioners.[22] It would be unlikely if the subject of steam navigation did not arise among the three men at that time.

At any rate, by 1815 an expedition, to be commanded by Capt. J. K. Tuckey RN, was being fitted out to explore the Zaire or Congo River – the hinterland of that part of Africa being then unknown to Europeans. The river was, however, known to be shallow – no more than a 4-foot draft would be allowed – and to flow strongly at its mouth, at six or seven knots. Banks's proposal was that the vessel being built for the expedition should be built as a steamboat, to counter the current, and to be fuelled by mangrove wood. The vessel was built under the supervision of the Surveyor of the Navy, and Boulton, Watt & Co. provided a neat little beam engine, no more than 13 feet high overall, to power it. Unfortunately, when the vessel was completed it was found that, as Tuckey put it, 'by some misconception the engine with its boiler was heavier, or the vessel drew more water, than had been anticipated'. Even after being lightened it drew 4 feet 3 inches and could achieve no more than 5½ knots. Engine and boiler were removed, and eventually used as a stationary engine in Chatham Dockyard; their space was used for stores and crew accommodation, and the Zaire River ascended successfully by the sea breeze and oars alone. Reading between the lines, one gets the impression that Tuckey was only too glad to have an excuse to get rid of this bulky piece of new and untried technology wished onto him from on high![23]

There were, however, two persons whose knowledge and opinions were respected by the naval authorities: Marc Isambard Brunel and John Rennie. It was to them as much as anyone that the successful introduction of steam power to the Royal Navy was due. The particular application was for steamboats to tow ships of war in and out of harbour when winds were contrary. Following representations by Brunel in 1816, arrangements were made for trials using the *Regent*. Some trials at least seem to have been made, although the Navy Board soon had a change of mind and disputed the cost of alterations made to the vessel.[24]

In 1819, however, Rennie reported at length to the Navy Board on the state of steam navigation, and made recommendations,[25] following which the then new Margate steam packet *Eclipse*, with a 60 hp Boulton, Watt & Co. engine, was set to tow the 74-gun line-of-battle ship *Hastings* downstream from Woolwich. After a few miles the tide proved too much for her, but nonetheless her potential had been demonstrated.[26]

The first consequence was that in 1821 the Navy purchased the HMS *Monkey*, built by Evans of Rotherhithe with a Boulton, Watt & Co. Engine.[27] Then, in November 1821, the first steamship to be built in a naval dockyard was laid down at Deptford. The name given to her, remarkably, was yet again *Comet*. She was built under the superintendence of Oliver

Lang, master shipwright of Woolwich Dockyard, who keenly supported Rennie's views. Her length was 115 feet between perpendiculars, her beam 21 feet 3 inches; Boulton, Watt & Co. supplied engines of 80 n.h.p. HMS *Comet* was launched on 23 May 1822. Her total cost, built and ready for sea, was £9,364. She had a long life ahead of her, for she was not broken up until 1868–9, having apparently served mainly as a tug or survey vessel, unarmed until 1830, after which guns of various types were fitted. Her boiler was replaced several times, but the original engine lasted until the end. It was then to be offered for sale – one would like to know the outcome.[28]

As early as August 1822 an occasion arose which enabled HMS *Comet* and other steamboats to give a convincing demonstration of their value for towing other vessels. This was the visit of King George IV to Scotland: he travelled north by sea, from Greenwich to Leith, aboard the royal yacht *Royal George*. For a start, the Lord Mayor of London, wishing to see his sovereign off with due ceremony, arranged to travel from the Tower to Greenwich in his own state barge – towed by one of Brocklebank's steamboats, the *Royal Sovereign*. At Greenwich spectators, and there were many, afloat and ashore, found the *Royal George* attended by not one but two steamers – HMS *Comet* and Brocklebank's east coast steamer *James Watt* – which were to accompany her north. The *James Watt* had in effect been press-ganged into service, her passengers, who had already gone aboard at Deptford, being transferred to another steamer, the *Tourist*. After His Majesty had embarked on the *Royal George* to the cheers of the multitude, she moved off, under tow by HMS *Comet*. The two steamers then accompanied the royal yacht, and the other eight sailing vessels which formed the royal squadron, on their way north. They towed the royal yacht, singly or together, or not according to whether the wind was fair for sailing. HMS *Comet* was also used for other purposes – to go off-shore from an overnight mooring to check on the sea conditions, for instance, and to take messengers ashore. Like this they reached Leith in four days – arrival was accompanied by the steamboat *Queen Margaret*, usually employed on the Queensferry passage, but on this day down the firth and crowded with spectators. The royal squadron eventually returned to Greenwich in the same manner.[29]

Construction of HMS *Comet* was followed in 1823 by construction, again at Deptford, of HMS *Lightning*, with engines by Maudslay. The following year she became the first steamer in the Royal Navy to take part in actual warfare.[30] From then on steam power spread slowly through the navy. Steam warships eventually appeared, even though as late as the 1840s it was considered that the proper role of a paddle steamer was to attend a sailing line-of-battleship, to tow her, or be towed, according to the state of the weather and the steamer's fuel bunkers.[31] By 1850 some seventy-seven paddle steamers of one sort or another had entered the service of the Royal Navy.[32]

Ocean voyages

The first steamship to cross the Atlantic was the *Savannah* in 1819, under the command of Moses Rogers, who had been associated with both Robert Fulton and John Stevens. But the *Savannah* was not so much a steamship as a sailing ship to which an auxiliary steam engine had been fitted, even though that engine was so bulky that, with its fuel supplies, it took up much of the interior of the hull. The crossing from Savannah to Liverpool took 27 days, 11 hours, of which the steam engine was in use for only about 3 days, 13 hours.[33] That encapsulates the problem of early ocean voyages by steamship: the steam plant was so bulky, and by later standards so inefficient, that sufficient coal could not be carried for a long voyage – and if, to carry more fuel, the hull were enlarged, then even more fuel would be needed, etc., etc. Or so it was believed. Early ocean voyages were made by a mix of sail and power.

The *Savannah* eventually returned across the Atlantic under sail alone, so the first east–west Atlantic crossing in which steam was used was that of the PS *Rising Star* in 1821, en route for South America.[34] The second such crossing was made in 1824–5, by the PS *Caroline*, the first steamer to serve in the French navy,[35] and another early Atlantic crossing was that made by PS *Curaçao*, which had been built on the Thames but sold to the Dutch Navy, in 1827.[36]

Using similar sail-and-steam techniques, the *Enterprize*, with a two-cylinder Maudslay side-lever engine, set out for India in 1825. With seventeen passengers and some cargo, she left Falmouth on 16 August. The engine was worked until 26 August, after which the fires were dropped, the paddle wheels locked with some floats removed, and while the ship sailed on the boiler was opened up and cleaned, and the cylinders opened up for the pistons to be adjusted. When all was ready the fires were lit again, and using sail and steam alternately, and at times together, she reached Cape Town on 13 October, and arrived at Calcutta on 7 December.[37]

The first steamer to reach the Arctic was the *Victory*, under command of Capt. John Ross, in search of the North-West Passage, in 1829.[38]

It took Isambard Kingdom Brunel, son of Marc Isambard, to realise that the ideas of the time on fuel capacity and hull size were not the whole story.

The capacity of a hull, he was aware, depended on its volume – on the cube of its dimensions – but its resistance, and thus the power needed to propel it, depended on its surface area, on the square of its dimensions. So if a steamship were built large enough, it would be able to carry enough coal for an Atlantic crossing under power.[39] The eventual outcome was the PS *Great Western* of 1838, 236 feet in length by 35 feet 3 inches beam. There were still 200 tons of coal on board when she reached New York on her maiden voyage from Bristol – a voyage which had taken 15 days and 5 hours.[40] At that period, the voyage by sailing packet could take 50 days. The evident rewards to be gained from accelerating the Atlantic crossing by using steam had led to a period of intense competition, with three companies vying for supremacy. None eventually would prove lasting, although the *Great Western* made seventy-four Atlantic crossings with great reliability,[41] but from this period emerged the formation in 1840 of the British and North American Royal Mail Steam Packet Co., for which its promoter Samuel Cunard was advised by Robert Napier to use much larger ships than he had at first envisaged.[42] The complex, heroic story of this period can scarcely be covered here in full, but it has been well told elsewhere.[43]

Iron hulls

Two other technological developments, both of which were vital for the continued development of the steamboat itself, were also reaching fruition at this time. They were the iron hull, and the screw propeller.

There had been intermittent attempts to make boats of iron since the late eighteenth century, and in 1819 the Forth & Clyde Canal company had the passage boat (horse-drawn) *Vulcan* built with a hull of iron, the better to resist winter ice. She was the outcome of the work of a committee appointed to consider reducing running expenses, upon which the distinguished members include James Watt and John Schank, and her builder Thomas Wilson pioneered techniques which would later become standard among builders of iron ships.[44]

The first steamboat to have an iron hull was the *Aaron Manby*, for which both hull and engine were built by Horseley Ironworks, Tipton, Staffordshire. Horseley had been building marine engines since 1817 at least; the vessel was named after Aaron Manby himself, who was 'master' of the ironworks, and her engine had two oscillating cylinders to his design. Otherwise the boat was very much the concern of his son Charles. Iron construction enabled her to be sent 'knocked down' by canal to Rotherhithe, where she was reassembled. Her eventual destination was Paris, reached under her own steam with Charles Manby as engineer, in June 1822. She was to make a valuable contribution to development of steamboat services on the Seine, and indirectly to French heavy industry when the Manbys founded important ironworks at Charenton near Paris. Here a second steamboat, delivered in parts, was reassembled, and here was made the engine for PS *Caroline*, mentioned above.[45]

A second iron-hulled steamboat, built by Horseley in around 1824, was sent in parts to Liverpool where she was erected. This was the *Marquis Wellesley*, ordered by John Grantham. Grantham was John Rennie's resident engineer who had surveyed the River Shannon in Ireland with a view to flood relief measures: from this he had come to appreciate its potential for steamer services, and with the *Marquis Wellesley* he established a steamer service on Lough Derg, part of the Shannon Navigation. He was bought out about 1829 by the Inland Steam Navigation Company, promoted by Charles Wye Williams, which in due course ordered an iron steamboat from William Laird at Birkenhead which was so large – 133 feet long and 17 feet wide – that she had to be transported in sections to the bank of Lough Derg at Killaloe for assembly there. This vessel, the *Lady Lansdowne*, was launched in 1833.[46] When eventually taken out of service, she was too large to leave the lough: her remains, in the recollection of the author, could still be found in a reed-bed at Killaloe as recently as the 1960s.

The first steamboat to be built on the Clyde with a hull of iron – or, more probably, an iron bottom and wooden sides – was the *Aglaia*, which David Napier placed on Loch Eck, Argyll, in 1827 – the author has told her story fully elsewhere.[47] The first iron-hulled steamer to ply on the Clyde proper was the *Fairy Queen* of 1831. John Neilson built her at Hamiltonhill, on the north side of Glasgow, and then, despite her 97-foot length and 8-foot beam, had her conveyed overland to the river. She plied between Glasgow, Largs and Millport, apparently successfully, overcoming a natural hesitation on the part of potential passengers to go aboard a vessel made of such a material.[48] From then on, iron shipbuilding on the Clyde progressed rapidly. In 1834, Tod & McGregor established a shipyard to build only ships of iron,[49] and between 1846 and 1852, of the 247 steamers built on the Clyde, only fourteen had hulls of wood.[50]

Screw propellers

The screw propeller is simple in concept, as pioneers of the early nineteenth century realised. Bringing it to practical form – combining pitch, diameter, number of blades, location, quantity, drive, speed, and other characteristics – proved far more difficult, as those pioneers soon discovered. After innumerable attempts had been made – as many as 470 names are said to have been associated with the invention – two men achieved success more or less simultaneously. One was John Ericsson, Swedish but resident at the time, 1836–7, in Britain. The other was Francis Pettit Smith. Ericsson left for the USA, whither some of his screw-driven vessels had preceded him, in 1839, leaving the field clear, in Britain, for Pettit Smith. Trials with a small steamboat, fitted with his form of propeller, were satisfactory, and the steamship *Archimedes* was completed in 1839, to tour the ports of Britain demonstrating it. When she reached Bristol in 1840 she was seized upon by Isambard Kingdom Brunel, who was then building, of iron, the *Great Western*'s even larger successor the *Great Britain*. After extensive trials of *Archimedes*, he concluded that work on the *Great Britain*'s huge paddle engines, already part-complete, must be suspended, and the ship built with screw propulsion instead.[51]

The seal was set on the success of the screw propeller, at least in the public eye, in 1845 when HMS *Rattler*, the Royal Navy's first screw-driven warship, was attached stern-to-stern to the paddle-driven HMS *Alecto*. The *Alecto* was set going full ahead, towing *Rattler*. When the *Rattler*'s engine was set going, the *Alecto* was first brought to a stand, and eventually towed astern at 2.8 knots.[52]

The screw propeller needed the iron hull, which unlike wood could withstand the stresses and vibration to which large propeller-driven ships are subject.[53] Certainly paddle-wheel propulsion would continue to be used in specialised situations – estuary steamers, for instance, which needed to stop smartly, by going astern, at one pier after another.[54] But it was the emergence of the screw propeller and the iron hull, and subsequently the steel hull and the compound engine, the triple expansion engine,[55] and the steam turbine, which allowed the steamship to reach its definitive form in the late Victorian and Edwardian eras. It was familiar to everyone, carrying passengers and freight around the world. Henry Bell's work had laid the foundations for this, and indeed for subsequent development of power-driven ships.

TEN

What Became of Bell – and What Became of the Comet

As he grew old, Henry Bell's health deteriorated. He became both lame and infirm – this seems to have been a consequence of over-exertion when in his prime. A particular problem was a knee wound, which never fully healed, and which had been incurred while installing a boiler into a steamboat. The effects of ill-health were showing as early as 1819.[1] Nevertheless, they did not prevent him from establishing the *Comet* on her west coast route, and simultaneously forwarding comprehensive proposals for improved docks at Glasgow to the Clyde Navigation Trustees. These included a canal along the north bank, and new docks at Glasgow Green, leaving the Broomielaw clear for the many steamboats by then using it. Perhaps over-ambitious, these proposals were not taken up.[2]

To return to Bell's health and circumstances: it is only possible to guess at the effect on him of the losses of first one, then the second, and finally the third of the three steamboats with which he was closely associated. But for more than sixty people to be killed in the tragedy of the second *Comet* as a result (however indirect) of an activity which he had originated amid high hopes – that would do nothing for anyone's peace of mind. Nor, doubtless, did those losses do anything for Bell's finances.[3]

Notoriously, Bell never settled in full with John Robertson, or David Napier, or John Wood, for the work they did towards the first *Comet*. The promissory notes he issued to them were never fully honoured.[4] This has caused a good deal of tut-tutting down the years. Yet it is worth having another look. When he originally ordered the *Comet*, Bell could reasonably have expected to pay off debts incurred during construction out of the eventual profits from operation. But Wood, soon after completing the *Comet,* built two more steamboats which were to be run in competition with her. One of these was run by Robertson, and Napier too became a Clyde steamboat operator before many years were out. Each of these, by his actions, was reducing the ability of Bell to pay what he owed. But more than that, each of them, during the steamboat boom which ensued, benefited greatly. In terms of business which came to them, in consequence of Bell's pioneering work, they profited to an extent which must have far exceeded the specific sums which Bell still owed to them. Certainly they seem to have been magnanimous toward his lack of payment.

Sometime in the 1820s Henry Bell re-visited his childhood home at Torphichen Mill, with a view to purchasing the land, building a second cottage, and retiring there.[5] But this plan did not come to fruition, and he continued to reside at the Baths Inn. Under Margaret Bell's capable management, this became the principal inn in the district, a favourite with Glaswegians visiting the coast.[6] As time went by, she had more and more to manage her husband's business affairs too.[7]

Sometime in the early 1820s also the public debt to Bell was recognised by the members of the civic authority in Glasgow, that is the Lord Provost, Magistrates and Council, acting in their capacity as trustees of the Clyde Navigation, who voted unanimously to make him an annuity of £50.[8] He was honoured in 1823 when the name *Henry Bell* was applied to a new fast steamboat for passengers and goods on the Glasgow–Liverpool run.[9] That might have been an empty honour, had not in the spring of 1826 a Mr Edward Morris, en route back to the land of his birth, taken passage on her at Liverpool for Glasgow.[10] Intrigued initially by the name, Morris was to become an enthusiastic and active champion for Bell – one whom he much needed, for this was the period of great controversy over responsibility for the origins of steamboats, controversy which was enhanced by the straightened circumstances of those who might have a share in it, and who could look to the government for a financial reward for benefits conferred on the public.

The flame of controversy had been ignited in 1822 by the fifth report from the House of Commons Select Committee on Holyhead Roads. In the opening pages of the committee's report on its inquiry into 'the important subject of Steam Boats' it gave much of the credit for their origination to Bell, more unfortunately than he deserved, for it stated among other things that he had 'given the first model of them to Mr Fulton' and had gone to America to assist him. Patrick Miller, by contrast, got only a passing mention, and so did William Symington. James Taylor, who considered he had played a vital role in proposing steam propulsion to Miller, got no mention at all.[11]

The consequence was that over the next few years Symington, Taylor and Bell, and their supporters, busied themselves in addressing petitions for financial reward, and justifying their claims, to whichever person highly-placed in government seemed most appropriate. This was done against a backdrop of claims and counter-claims: they were made public, supported by affidavits from anyone who, it seemed, might have a clear recollection of events, in increasingly vituperative and detailed pamphlets and letters to the press. Symington was eventually rewarded, about 1825, to the extent of a grant of £100 from the privy purse, followed by a further £50 a year or two later. Bell eventually received a small reward too, as mentioned below. Taylor died in 1825, but his widow received an annual pension of £50 and his four daughters each received a gift of £50 as late as 1837. Patrick Miller had died in 1815 and would scarcely have needed financial support anyway. That did not prevent his son, Patrick Miller junior, taking up the cudgels on his behalf, and a descendant published a pamphlet on this subject as late as 1862, so long did this controversy rumble on. Looking back from the best part of two centuries later, it all seems rather sterile – except that, as Harvey and Downs Rose point out, it is to the pamphlets and articles to which it gave rise, and indeed to the biographies of Symington and Bell which emerged from it, that we now owe much of our knowledge of these events. The difficulty remains to distinguish what is exaggerated from what is accurate.[12]

During the summer of 1826 Edward Morris, having decided to take up Bell's cause, wrote a series of letters to the Glasgow newspapers. In these, after eloquently recounting Bell's achievements and circumstances, he urged 'the leading gentlemen of all parties in politics and religion (for Bell is our common benefactor) to make an appeal to government or to parliament on his behalf'. To these he added 'Steam-boat proprietors of Glasgow, and engineers and builders of these magnificent barques' who were 'emphatically Bell's debtors', urging their support. These letters were copied in Edinburgh and Liverpool papers. The outcome was, according to Morris, that thirty-five towns and counties in Scotland sent petitions to the government to grant Bell a pension.[13]

On the strength of these, Bell in 1827 travelled to London – which, with his deteriorating health, must have been for him no small undertaking – and had an interview with the Prime Minister, George Canning, in person. There was only limited result. Canning wrote an order to the Treasury to make a single payment to Bell, of £200, and Bell returned home. Reading between the lines, one gets the impression that Canning may well have been aware that claims to have originated steam navigation had by then become a contentious matter. At any rate, friends of Bell in Glasgow advised against collecting this payment, while a further attempt was made to persuade Canning to make it an annual sum. But shortly afterwards Canning unfortunately died in office, from pneumonia. Two years passed before Bell eventually received the grant, and then only when one of his friends – probably Morris himself – visited the Treasury and arranged payment.[14]

Earlier, it seems, Clyde steamboat proprietors had offered to Henry Bell the proceeds of a day's sailing of all their boats, to be repeated annually. This offer Bell, hoping for a government pension, had refused.[15] But after returning empty-handed from London, he consented in December 1828 to a public subscription in his favour in Glasgow, Liverpool and other places. Morris obtained the support of many prominent people in Glasgow, London and elsewhere for this; some £500 was in due course raised, and the Clyde Navigation trustees upped Bell's pension to £100 a year.[16]

Among those from whom Morris had obtained expressions of support – and no doubt subscriptions too – he listed Thomas Telford, Thomas Rhodes (who had worked under Telford on the Caledonian Canal and St Katherine's Docks in London, and went on to become engineer for the Shannon Navigation improvements of the 1830s and 40s) and 'Sir Isambard Brunel'. This was Marc Isambard Brunel, distinguished engineer in his own right and father of an even more distinguished son, Isambard Kingdom Brunel. Morris called on him in 1829 in London, where he was engaged in driving a tunnel beneath the Thames. His support was given willingly.[17] It appears to have been on this occasion that Marc Isambard Brunel commented to Morris: 'Bell did what we engineers all failed in – he gave us the sea-steamer; his scheming was Britain's steaming.'[18]

Although Henry Bell's physical health was failing, his mind remained as active as ever. At the end of August 1830 he made public, through the medium of an open letter 'To the Gentlemen, Freeholders and Merchants of Argyleshire', a detailed and costed scheme for a canal across the Kintyre peninsula from Tarbert to West Loch Tarbert. This he had been maturing for a couple of years. The idea of a canal over the route was not new: it had been considered in the 1770s, when the Crinan Canal was proposed, as an alternative and rejected because of the narrowness of West Loch Tarbert and the difficulty of its navigation by sailing ships in contrary winds. By 1830 the development of steamboats had removed this objection. And to Bell, with personal experience of operating steamboats through the Crinan Canal, the inadequacies of that waterway must have been all too clear. Its locks and other structures had been built to dimensions suitable for small coasting sailing vessels of the 1790s. As new steamboats of ever increasing size came into general use, these dimensions were to become increasingly restrictive, and from the 1840s it was to become the practice to divide up the Glasgow–Oban route into three stages – using full-sized steamers between Glasgow and Ardrishaig, and Crinan and Oban, and carrying passengers through the canal by horse-drawn track boats, initially, and later by the little canal steamer *Linnet*. Bell's Tarbert proposal of 1830 was for a full-size ship canal, free from locks and of large dimensions. This he anticipated would be used not only by coasting vessels but by transatlantic shipping. It was to be funded by formation of a joint-stock company.[19]

Such proposals take time to mature, and Bell did not live to see formation of the Argyll Canal Company, and passage of an Act of Parliament to make a canal over this route, in 1846. But capital proved impossible to raise. It may or may not be coincidence that this was the time of the growth and collapse of the speculative bubble that was the railway mania. The company was dissolved in 1849.[20] The subject got a further airing at the time of the Royal Commission on Canals and Waterways of 1906, as an alternative to enlargement of the Crinan Canal, by then much needed.[21] But it did not come to fruition, neither was the Crinan Canal enlarged, and the bottleneck that canal represents has continued to bedevil west-of-Scotland communications ever since. In this, his last scheme, however, Bell's vision had once again homed in accurately on a need, a demand, a potential and the means to fulfil it.

By the time he prepared his Tarbert canal scheme, Henry Bell was already largely bed-ridden. He eventually passed away, at the Baths Inn, on 14 November 1830. Edward Morris provides an eye-witness of his funeral procession, on 19 November, when despite wet and stormy weather a large crowd accompanied the hearse from the Baths Inn past closed shops to the church at Rhu (or Row as it was then known) and 140 people attended the funeral.[22] Row was the parish in which Helensburgh had been established; by the end of Bell's life, Helensburgh's year-round population had risen to about 1,000, and in summer, thanks to summer visitors brought by steamboats, to three times that number.[23]

Remarkably, Bell's grave went unmarked for many years, Margaret Bell having been advised that others wished to commemorate him appropriately. Eventually, in 1853, it was at the expense of Robert Napier that it was surmounted by the large and imposing statue of Henry Bell, seated, which is still prominent in Rhu churchyard to this day.[24] Margaret Bell continued to receive a pension from the Clyde navigation trustees, although it reverted from £100 per year to £50,[25] and continued to run the Baths Inn until her own death in 1856.[26]

John Robertson too fell on hard times. Having initially profited greatly from his steamboats to the extent of accumulating over £9,000, his liabilities came to exceed his assets and he was declared bankrupt in 1826; he eventually settled with his creditors to the extent of paying ten shillings in the pound. He then seems to have become largely dependent on the generosity of friends,[27] but would have one further moment of glory, mentioned below.

The engine which Robertson had supplied for the *Comet* in 1812 survived, eventually to reach the Science Museum in London, although the course of events by which it did so was far from straightforward. After removal from the *Comet* in 1819[28] it was sold for further use on land. The purchaser was Archibald McLellan & Son, Glasgow coachbuilder, and Bell may have provided it to discharge a debt for a coach they had supplied. At any rate, it was used to drive lathes, grindstones and so on in McLellan's works, which it did for some time, until Robertson was commissioned to buy it by a Mr Alexander, distiller of Greenock, which he was able to do for £60. It subsequently passed through several hands, and by the late 1830s had been acquired by Charles Atherton, manager of Claud Girdwood & Co., engineers who built much machinery for bucket dredgers for the Clyde Navigation trustees. It was exhibited to the British Association when it met in Glasgow in 1840, and was subsequently displayed at Glasgow Polytechnic, until the building was destroyed by fire in 1855. On this occasion the engine fell from the top floor and was buried in the debris.[29]

That might have been the end of the story, had it not been for Bennet Woodcroft. Woodcroft was author of *A Sketch of the Origin and Progress of Steam Navigation* (1848), a vital source of information on the subject. He is perhaps better known as the 'father of the Patent Office'. No ordinary civil servant, but one of independent spirit and immense energy, he successfully reformed archaic procedures for patenting inventions, and in the process established the Patent Office Museum. This became the forerunner of the Science Museum. By 1860 Woodcroft's curator at the Patent Office Museum was Francis Pettit Smith, pioneer of the screw propeller. Woodcroft had some patents in that field himself.[30]

The museum's collection had originated with the models submitted by applicants for patents; Woodcroft was assiduous in seeking out artefacts which represented advances in technology to add to them. With a minimal budget, however, he was dependent on the generosity of donors.[31] During the 1850s he had organised a successful eleventh-hour rescue of Symington's Dalswinton steamboat engine of 1788.[32] In 1861, he turned his attention to seeking out the engine of the *Comet*. In this he enlisted the help of noted engineer John Scott Russell, and it was through Russell's agency that in July

1862 the engine was located, rusty and neglected, in the yard of a Glasgow engine builder. Instructing Pettit Smith to get the engine as soon as possible, Woodcroft proposed seeking the assistance of another contact, Thomas Lloyd, Engineer-in-Chief to the navy, who was in a position to determine which Clyde shipyards received orders. If the engine's owners proved to be engine builders, wrote Woodcroft, Smith should ask Lloyd to approach them also. As Woodcroft put it: 'Those who make engines for the Admiralty wish to continue to do so. Those who do not would be very glad to begin.'[33]

In fact the owners of the *Comet* engine, William Craig & Co., were in liquidation, and it was Robert Napier & Sons who came to the rescue. Robert Napier himself was by this date the doyen of Clyde shipbuilders and had taken his sons into partnership. The manager of Napiers' Glasgow works, Thomas Carswell, was instrumental in acquiring the engine. When he started negotiations with Craig & Co.'s liquidators he learned that they had already received an offer of £20 for the engine, probably for scrap. Nevertheless, he successfully persuaded them to allow Napiers first refusal. At that point the foreman of the yard in which the engine was stored evidently woke up to the fact that what had appeared to be a pile of rusting iron was something of importance, and offered £25 himself. Carswell came back with an offer of £50. This was accepted, paid, and a receipt given. But when Napiers sent a gang of men with a cart to the yard to collect the engine, the foreman turned them away. On a second attempt the same thing happened, and it was only at the third attempt that the engine was successfully collected and taken to Napiers' works.

Napiers cleaned up the engine and straightened out parts which had been damaged in the 1855 fire. Carswell made contact with John Robertson, by then aged at least 80, and that November he came to Napiers' works and proudly posed beside his engine for photographs. There remained the problem of getting the engine to South Kensington. This was solved when Pettit Smith persuaded the west coast railway companies to carry it to Euston free of charge.

Robert Napier & Sons presented the *Comet* engine to the Patent Office Museum. They did more: they arranged for John Robertson himself to travel to London to set it up. The old man travelled to London by overnight train and arrived shortly before Christmas. Happily, he worked on re-erecting in the museum the engine which he himself had built so long before. But he could not be persuaded to stay in London a moment longer than necessary, even though many in the engineering profession would have liked to hear him speak of his recollections. He signed a statement to authenticate the engine, and set off home again, arriving back in Glasgow exhausted but in time for Hogmanay.[34]

The engine of the *Comet* continues to be displayed in the Science Museum, and to show the feature which confirms its authenticity (if any were needed), that is that the cylinder is conspicuously over-size for the cast iron framework which supports it. It will be recalled that the original cylinder, of 11 ½-inch diameter, was replaced after a few months use by one of 12½-inch diameter; and to this day the lower flange of the cylinder on the engine, and two of the flange bolts also, can be observed to overlap the framework.[35]

The original 11½-diameter cylinder has also survived. Bell evidently retained it, and Mrs Bell adopted it as a coal-scuttle. She eventually presented it to Andrew Macgeorge, the author who included her recollection of the *Comet*'s being pushed off a shoal – mentioned above – in his book *Old Glasgow*. He was prevailed upon in 1862 to lend it to the Science Museum, but twelve years later requested its return.[36] It passed into the Glasgow Museums collection, and was latterly loaned to the Scottish Maritime Museum, but has now returned to Glasgow again and is displayed in the Riverside Museum.

Perhaps Bennet Woodcroft was motivated to go in search of the *Comet*'s engine by the approach of the *Comet*'s fiftieth anniversary in 1862. That remains uncertain. There is no uncertainty over the enthusiasm and scale of the *Comet*'s centenary celebrations in 1912. That August, on the banks of the Clyde, there were no less than 134 ships under construction in twenty-eight shipyards. They included six battleships and the liner *Aquitania* which, when complete, would be the largest ship afloat. A fleet of little steamers carried passengers up, down and across river and firth, whether they were on business or, more particularly, pleasure bent. To the paddle steamers, by then traditional, there had been added a few years earlier turbine steamers, which were world leaders in technology. The prosperity of the region was clear for all to see, and everyone knew that the true progenitor of this prosperity was Henry Bell.

An executive committee was formed to arrange centenary celebrations: it had Glasgow's Lord Provost as its convenor, included ten more representatives of Glasgow Corporation, and thirty-three other members who represented bodies ranging from the councils of surrounding towns to organisations such as the Clyde Navigation Trust, Glasgow University, and the Institution of Engineers and Shipbuilders in Scotland, to some of the principal shipbuilders. The main celebrations took place over 29, 30 and 31 August, the last of which dates was declared a public holiday.

The programme for the event was a 128-page hardback.[37] Highlights included illuminated and decorated cars on the city's electric tramway system on 29 August, and a formal luncheon in the City Chambers on

30 August – those present heard the Rt Hon. T. M'Kinnon Wood MP, Secretary for Scotland, deliver a eulogy on Henry Bell. The climax came on 31 August with a review of shipping assembled beyond the Tail of the Bank. Long lines of ships gathered to honour the memory of Henry Bell and the *Comet* stretched from Greenock to Helensburgh. There were a dozen ships from the Royal Navy – battleships, cruisers and destroyers – commanded by Admiral Sir John Jellicoe. There were liners, merchant vessels and yachts. Not forgotten were the Clyde's own essential dredgers, hopper barges and tugs. The official party of prominent citizens and dignitaries set out from the Broomielaw at noon, on board the *Columba*, the most elegant and famous of all the Clyde paddle steamers. Eleven other steamers followed the *Columba* from Glasgow, and more vessels of all sizes joined in as she went down river. When they reached the assembled ships, they passed up and down the eight lanes between them, in a procession so long that while the *Columba* was half-way up one lane, the tail-end was still only half-way down the previous one. The day was rounded off by a display of fireworks on Glasgow Green.

At the same time, Kelvingrove Museum hosted an extensive temporary exhibition of material relating to Bell, the *Comet* and other early steamboats.[38] The numerous exhibits included portraits of inventors and pioneers, a photograph of the Baths Hotel, Henry Bell's business card and promissory notes, pictures of steamboats and the Clyde, models of ships, boilers and engines, drawings of engines, boilers and machinery, ephemera and tourist guides, and seven volumes of documents collected by Bennet Woodcroft which were loaned by the Patent Office Library.

Other local towns held their own celebrations on 31 August, particularly Port Glasgow and Helensburgh, and some 130 harbour towns all round Scotland displayed flags and bunting to mark the occasion. At Neilston, birthplace of John Robertson, a granite obelisk in his memory was unveiled on 24 August, and at Torphichen Mill, birthplace of Henry Bell, a memorial tablet was attached to the ruin of the remaining building on 4 November.

The one thing that was missing from the 1912 celebrations was a full-size representation of the *Comet*. For that, the world had to wait for the 150th anniversary celebrations in 1962. Firm planning for that event started only in March 1962, the leading light being Provost Walter P. Lucas, who had taken part in the centenary celebrations in 1912. Exhibitions and parades were planned, but a centrepiece connected with the original vessel was needed. A statue? A monument? A model? Ah – a replica, a full-size working replica – from the moment that was proposed, the project seems to have taken off, becoming a remarkable spontaneous community effort. Of the most important components, only the wooden hull was built elsewhere, by G. Thomson of Buckie. Local companies did the rest – the engine was built by John G. Kincaid & Co. Ltd., the boiler by Rankin & Blackmore Ltd, and the vessel was engined and fitted out at Lithgows Ltd's yard, with the strong support of Sir William Lithgow. Some twenty-five local firms are recorded as having helped.

Detail design work on the engine was entrusted to Kincaid's chief draughtsman, Andrew Mumford. He travelled to the Science Museum to measure and examine closely the original engine, although the museum authorities would not permit the cylinder or valve casing to be opened for fear of damage, because the metal was believed to have become brittle. A wagon-type boiler was provided to work at a maximum pressure of 10 lb per sq. in. The replica *Comet* was complete enough to be photographed while being fitted out afloat at Lithgows on 27 August. She was then hauled out again.

The ceremonial naming ceremony and launch took place at Lithgows Ltd's East Yard soon after 12.30 p.m. on 1 September 1962. After lunch, and a mile-long procession of decorated floats through the town, the official party of fourteen notables, all dressed in early nineteenth-century costume, went aboard her at Kingston Basin. They included Mr W. Bell, great-grand nephew of Henry Bell. The replica *Comet* then set out for Helensburgh, satisfactorily although slowly, and accompanied by innumerable small craft. At Helensburgh the official party visited the Queen's Hotel for a light meal: that was Henry Bell's Baths Inn, renamed. By the time the replica *Comet* returned to Port Glasgow that evening, in the rain and after dark, 15,000 people were waiting to welcome her.

Over the next two weeks, more than 7,000 people paid to visit the *Comet* in Kingston Basin. The Comet Trust Fund was set up to build a home for her and provide travelling scholarships for shipbuilding apprentices. But euphoria evaporates, and neither goal was achieved. The replica was stored under cover until 1974, when she was loaned to the Burgh of Port Glasgow, which placed her on display at a location near the town centre and close to where the original was built. In 1983 Inverclyde District Council, which had succeeded the Burgh of Port Glasgow, accepted the replica *Comet* from Scott Lithgow as a gift, together with the £2,800 remaining in the trust fund, to be used towards repairs. Repairs to the hull in fact cost considerably more than this; they had become necessary because, although the vessel was displayed in the centre of an ornamental pond, this was insufficient to keep intruders from going aboard. The interior had to be cleaned and fumigated before repair work could start.[39]

Some more repairs were done in 1998, but by 2010 the vessel was in poor condition and needed refurbishment. With the bicentenary approaching, Inverclyde Council (which had inherited the replica *Comet* following a further reorganisation of local government) allocated £180,000 towards the task from its Common Good Fund. This was sufficient only for materials, however, and further support was obtained from the UK Government's Future Jobs Fund programme to pay labour costs. That enabled work to go ahead, organised by a partnership of Inverclyde Council, Inverclyde Community Development Trust and Ferguson Shipbuilders, with the combined intention of creating local employment and preserving a really important part of the community heritage.

The replica was lifted and taken to Ferguson's yard, Port Glasgow, where the work of refurbishment was done by local young people learning boatbuilding skills. Two successive groups of eight people took part, with one more person whose task was to record and photograph the project. The principal task of the main groups was replacement of the many rotten timbers, in hull, deck, and paddle boxes; the housing of the aft cabin was completely replaced. To gain access to rotten woodwork, the engine was lifted out, and subsequently replaced. The cabins were tidied up but the vessel was not restored internally. A full re-paint then followed. While the work was going on, staff from the trust visited every school in Port Glasgow to tell pupils about their heritage in the *Comet*, and every school sent a delegation of pupils to visit the site and see the work for themselves. In June 2011 the refurbished replica *Comet* was returned to her place, the centrepiece of the town centre.

Available funding did not, regrettably, extend to making the vessel seaworthy again or to operating her afloat on the occasion of the bicentenary. On the other hand, it is said to be sufficient to provide a canopy over her, something which for decades has been conspicuous by its absence. This was out to tender at the time of writing, late in 2011. It will probably prove more important, than a brief period of operation, for the long-term security of a replica which is fast becoming a historic vessel in its own right.[40]

APPENDIX

What is Left Today

Some relics of Bell, the *Comet* and some other early steamboats are to be found at the following locations:

Science Museum, Exhibition Road, London SW7 2DD
Engine of the *Comet*, displayed in gallery 'Making the Modern World'.
Also in the collection, but probably not on display in the latter part of 2012 and in 2013 because of gallery re-organisation: oil painting of *Comet* on the Forth, attributed to Alexander Nasmyth; rigged model of *Comet*; engine from Symington's Dalswinton boat of 1788.

Riverside Museum, 100 Pointhouse Place, Glasgow, G3 8RS
Display case of artefacts relating to Bell and the *Comet* including: portrait of Henry Bell; portrait of John Robertson; bust of David Napier; builder's model of *Comet*; original 11½-inch diameter cylinder from *Comet*'s engine; *Comet*'s compass and ship's bell recovered from wreck; account book with details of salvage attempts at Craignish; table ordered by Bell for *Comet*, one of three of which this one was left on the joiner's hands. It is proposed to add an audio-visual screen to interpret the account book. Display case containing relics of *Charlotte Dundas*, including pieces of timber cut from the second boat's hull when laid up and disintegrating. Engine (1828) from steamboat *Industry*. Engine said to be from the second *Comet* but of doubtful authenticity – found in 1877 driving a paint mill in Glasgow (ref. Mitchell Library, Wotherspoon Collection, vol. I, p. 88), it is of similar layout to the engine of the first *Comet* – of great interest as a very early

portable steam engine and, in the author's view, likely to have been built by John Robertson.

Glasgow Museums Resource Centre, 200 Woodhead Road, South Nitshill Industrial Estate, Glasgow G53 7NN

Open to the public, but all visits must be booked in advance: see website www.glasgowlife.org.uk

Half-models of many early steamboats, and other related records and artefacts.

Torphichen, West Lothian

Church: Memorial plaque to Henry Bell.

Ruin of Torphichen Mill (Bell's birthplace) with commemorative plaque, OS grid ref. NS 956737, on south bank of river. Adjoins River Avon Heritage Trail long-distance path, but difficult of access in 2011 as path in part closed and in any case lacking access from roads in the vicinity. West Lothian Council has advised the author of plans to reopen the path and to make a link from Torphichen village.

Southern Necropolis, Caledonia Road, Gorbals, Glasgow

Grave of John Robertson with memorial, not visited by author but clear instructions for finding it available in 2011 from website www.southernnecropolis.co.uk

Neilston, Renfrewshire

Obelisk in memory of John Robertson, with inlaid representation of *Comet*'s engine, located in the angle between High Street and Kirkstyle Lane.

Port Glasgow, town centre, close to A8 Greenock Road

Full-size replica *Comet*, with interpretative board, displayed near where both it and the original were built.

McLean Museum and Art Gallery, 15 Kelly Street, Greenock, PA16 8JX

Carvings recovered from wreck of second *Comet*. Oil paintings of Queen Victoria's visit to the Clyde, 1847.

Dunglass Point, Bowling

Overlooking Clyde, large monument to Henry Bell, on private land and apparently inaccessible to public.

Dumbarton, Denny Tank (part of Scottish Maritime Museum)
Engine from PS *Leven*, 1828.

Helensburgh
East Clyde Street, on south side between street and shore, original building of Bell's Baths Inn, later the Queens Hotel and now part of a larger development.

East Clyde Street, south side closer to pier, displayed out of doors, flywheel from *Comet* (said to be the original, replaced during modifications) and anvil used by Bell's blacksmith.

West Clyde Street, south side, prominent red granite obelisk put up in memory of Bell, 1872.

Rhu, churchyard, entry from Church Road off A814 Gareloch Road, parking in churchyard.
Memorial to Henry Bell, large seated figure over his and Margaret Bell's grave.

Iron gravestone, horizontal, third row on left from entrance, provided by Bell to mark grave of Capt. Bain of *Comet*.

Dalswinton House, Dumfriesshire, DG2 0XZ
Full-size replica of 1788 boat displayed under canopy adjacent to loch where trials of the original were done. (refs.: *Scotland on Sunday*, 26 April 2009, gardens section, 24; website www.dalswintonestate.co.uk consulted 28 Jan. 2012)

Notes and References

Abbreviations used below:
GMRC: Glasgow Museums Resource Centre
JRCHS: *Journal of the Railway and Canal Historical Society*
NAS: National Archives of Scotland
NLS: National Library of Scotland
MPICE: *Minutes of Proceedings of the Institution of Civil Engineers*
ODNB: *Oxford Dictionary of National Biography*
TNS: *Transactions of the Newcomen Society*

Chapter One:
The First Powered Transport

1. Stationary steam engines had earlier been applied to haulage of
    goods waggons up the inclined planes of tramroads.
2. Hamilton, 1–2, 213–23.
3. Riddell, 73.
4. Baedeker, 538.
5. Thomson, 15; Bell, 16.
6. For Watt's relationship with Roebuck, see Watters, 28–32. The early
    development of the steam engine generally is well covered by Hills,
    and by Dickinson and Jenkins.
7. *A Biographical Dictionary of Civil Engineers...* 554–69; Boucher,
    6–13; Hills, 70–2.

8. Birse, 43–5.
9. Dickinson and Jenkins, 346.
10. Hills, 70.
11. Hamilton, 210.
12. Dickinson and Jenkins, 321.
13. Rolt, 1962, 76–81; Scott, 11–13, 33–43. Rolt refers to Watt's and Boulton's activities as 'commercial brigandage'.
14. Hills, 81; Rolt, 74; Scott, 48.
15. Day and McNeil, 509; Rolt, 1962, 72.
16. Hills, 116.
17. Scott, 10, 24.
18. Murray, M., 'Description of a Portable Steam Engine' in Nicholson, W., *A Journal of natural philosophy, chemistry and the arts* new series vol. XI, 1805, 93–5, plate 7; Rolt, 73; Scott, 13, 62, plate 4.

Chapter Two:
Steamboats Before Bell

1. Spratt, 1958, 23.
2. Woodcroft, 1.
3. Spratt, 1958, 26; Woodcroft, 11.
4. Spratt, 1958, 38–9.
5. Oldham, J., 'On the Rise, Progress, and present Position of Steam Navigation in Hull', in Report of the 23rd meeting of the British Association for the Advancement of Science, Hull, 1853, 46–7; Woodcroft, 123; correspondence between the author and Derek Grindell.
6. Harvey & Downs Rose, 13–15, 24–5; Ransom, 1984, 75.
7. Hamilton 8, 155 *et seq.*; ODNB, article on Miller, Patrick, website www.oxforddnb.com consulted 16 Dec. 2010; Purcell Taylor collection, Mitchell Library, Glasgow, accession no. 599617; Ransom, 1984, 75.
8. Woodcroft, 32–5.
9. Spratt, 1958, 49; *The Official Catalogue…of the Great Exhibition…*1473.
10. Controversy over performance of Dalswinton boat: for Nasmyth, see Woodcroft, 40; for Cleland, see Cleland 1825, 48. See also Harvey & Downs Rose, 51–3; Purcell Taylor collection, Mitchell Library, Glasgow, accession no. 599617; Spratt, 1958, 49.

11. Ransom, 1984, 75–7; Symington, 5.
12. Symington, 5–6; *The Official Catalogue...of the Great Exhibition...*1474–5; Woodcroft, 36–7.
13. Woodcroft, 37.
14. Woodcroft, 44–5.
15. Purcell Taylor collection, Mitchell Library, Glasgow, accession no. 599617; Tann, 337.
16. Dickinson & Jenkins, 318.
17. *The Official Catalogue...of the Great Exhibition...*1475.
18. Spratt, 1958, 29, 36.
19. Fitch's fascinating early career is well covered by Flexner, 19–37, 50–63.
20. Flexner, 76–8, 102–9, 122–6, 181–5; Prager, 191.
21. Flexner, 186–9.
22. See, e.g., Dickinson, 8.
23. Flexner, 67–8, 189.
24. Flexner, 68, 384.
25. Flexner, 91, 129–32, 142, 152–6, 163, 166–8, 174–6, 208–13; Spratt, 1958, 45–8
26. Flexner, 93–4, 147–8, 236–7.
27. *A Biographical Dictionary of Civil Engineers...*, 90; Spratt, 1958, 59.
28. Dickinson, 19; Philip, 22, 24.
29. Dickinson, 19–22.
30. Twenty new canals were authorised in 1793, compared with seven in 1792 and ten in 1794: Hadfield, *British Canals*, 1969, 106.
31. Dickinson, 22.
32. Dickinson, 223; Dyer, 286.
33. Flexner, 219.
34. Mitchell, 134.
35. Malet, 151.
36. Dickinson, 30.
37. Dickinson, 64–5.
38. Day & McNeil (eds.), 665.
39. Buchanan, viii; Flexner, 174; Spratt, 1958, 54–5; Stanhope & Gooch, 165–180.
40. *Mechanics' Magazine*, vol. xvii, 1832, 260.
41. Dickinson & Jenkins, 320.
42. Malet, 150–2; ODNB, article on Schank, John, website www.oxforddnb.com consulted on 16 December 2010.
43. Dickinson & Jenkins, 6, 42.

44. Woodcroft, 53.
45. Symington, 7.
46. E.g., Bowman and Harvey & Downs Rose differ greatly in their interpretations of the course of events during development of *Charlotte Dundas*; Spratt, 1958, and Lindsay, both sources which are generally reliable, fail to appreciate that there was more than one boat.
47. Rankine, 18–25.
48. Watters, 81, 87.
49. Recent accounts of Symington and the *Charlotte Dundas* appear in: Bowman, 10–23; Fox, 21–3; Harvey & Downs Rose, 117–139; Paterson, 96–9; Ransom, 1984, 79–82; *The first practical steamboat...*, 7–16.
50. Harvey & Downs Rose, 120.
51. NAS Carron Co. Invoice Book 1798–1801, ref. GD 58/4/19/26. (Future researchers may like to note that the reference GD58/6/26, which has been given elsewhere, is incorrect.)
52. Rankine, 5–6.
53. Rankine, 6.
54. According to eye-witness David Napier: Napier, 16–17.
55. Dickinson & Titley, 62.
56. Hamilton, 127–8; Lindsay, 38–9; Lindsay, J., 'Conflict and Conspiracy in the Forth & Clyde Navigation Company 1814–1816' in *Canal News* (Forth & Clyde Canal Society) no. 134, Feb. 2009, 8–10.
57. Skempton, A. W. 'A History of the Steam Dredger, 1797–1830' in TNS, vol. 47, 1974–6, 97–8.
58. *Mechanics' Magazine*, 23 August 1845, 113–120; Skempton, A. W. 'A History of the Steam Dredger, 1797–1830' in TNS, vol. 47, 1974–6, 98–103.
59. Hills, 97–9; Flexner, 267–8; Spratt 1958, 69–70; Woodcroft, 59–60.
60. Conditions in the Highlands at this period, and their complexities, are well summarised in Cameron, 5–21.
61. Lindsay, 146, 149.
62. 'Doughfour Loch': Loch Dochfour was a small loch adjoining the north-eastern end of Loch Ness. Its water level was eventually raised to that of its larger neighbour.
63. Second *Report of the Caledonian Canal Commissioners*, 1805, 33.
64. Third *Report of the Caledonian Canal Commissioners*, 1806, 3, 11, 25, 27; Fourth *Report...*, 1807, 63.

65. Skempton, A. W. 'A History of the Steam Dredger, 1797–1830' in TNS, vol. 47, 1974–6, 103.

66. Quoted in Gibb, 100.

67. An entire book has been devoted to the vexed question of Telford's relationship with Jessop: Hadfield, *Thomas Telford's Temptation.*

68. Skempton, A.W. 'William Chapman (1749–1832), Civil Engineer' in TNS, vol. 46, 1973–4, 46–7, 63–4.

69. Skempton, A. W. 'A History of the Steam Dredger, 1797–1830' in TNS, vol. 47, 1974–6, 104–5.

70. Twelfth *Report of the Caledonian Canal Commissioners*, 1815, 5; see also note 62 above.

71. Skempton, A. W. 'A History of the Steam Dredger, 1797–1830' in TNS, vol. 47, 1974–6, 111–2.

72. Fulton and his remarkable career are well described in Dickinson *Robert Fulton engineer and artist*, Flexner *Steamboats Come True*, and Philip *Robert Fulton: A Biography*. It is to these works that the present author is indebted for most of the facts which form the following summary of Fulton's career.

73. Dickinson, 213.

74. Dickinson, 147.

75. Rankine, 22–3; Woodcroft, 66.

76. Dickinson 179–81; Fox 25–7; Ransom, 1984, 92–3. It has often been suggested that Fulton must have gone to see the *Charlotte Dundas* after he returned to Britain in 1804. The earliest his other commitments, which are mentioned later in chapter two, would have permitted would have been late in that year, by which date Boulton, Watt & Co. were already making engine components for the *Clermont*, so that a visit then would have had limited value, while in any case *Charlotte Dundas* is likely to have been laid up.

77. Dickinson, plate opposite p. 152; Spratt, 1958, 65–6.

78. ODNB, article 'Watt, James, (1769–1848)' consulted on website www.oxforddnb.com on 23 Jan. 2012.

79. Dickinson, 168–79.

80. Dickinson, 215–21; Flexner, 320–6; Philip, 191, 193, 198–203; Spratt, 1958, 75–6.

81. Dickinson, 221–9.

82. Flexner, 266–7, 333–5; Spratt, 1958, 76–7.

83. Bellico, 154–5, 186; ODNB, article 'Schank, John' consulted on website www.oxforddnb.com on 16 Dec. 2010.

84. Beach, 79–81; Bellico, 258–61; Spratt, 1958, 77–8.

85. Spratt, 1958, 81–5; Tann & Macleod, 18.
86. Flexner, 341–3; Philip, 270–1, 275–6; Spratt, 1958, 85–6.
87. Day & McNeil (eds.), 226–7; Dyer, 287, 291–2.

Chapter Three:
Henry Bell Himself

1. Morris, 15–16, 23; Osborne, B., 45–8. A detailed paper on the genealogy of the Bell family from the seventeenth century to the twentieth, prepared in 1996 by family member I. L. G. Baillie, is held in GMRC, Research Files relevant to Bell and the *Comet*. Bell's date of birth is given as 7 April 1767 in Morris, 16, quoting Bell himself, and this date is generally accepted. However a certified copy birth certificate is held in GMRC, Research Files relevant to Bell and the *Comet*: this gives the date of birth as 7 April 1768 and states, in the original spelling, 'To Patrick Bell and Margrate Easton in Torphichen Millen a son baptised called Hendrey'. Bell, D., in Napier, 81, is dismissive of this, stating that the entry occurs in the records of 1768 in the Parish Register but has evidently been interpolated at a date later than the entries which precede and follow it. He suggests it is a record of baptism, not birth.
2. *A Biographical Dictionary of Civil Engineers...* 204–5; Gibb, 95; MPICE vol. XIV, session 1854–5, 131–2 (Memoir of Alexander Easton).
3. Morris, 16; Osborne, B., 1995, 48.
4. Morris, 16; Osborne, B., 1995, 54–5. Morris quotes Bell as saying that he went to Shaw & Hart to be 'instructed in ship modelling'. Bell was, presumably, using the verb 'model' in the first, and obsolete, meaning given to it the *New Shorter Oxford English Dictionary*: 'Draw a plan of; produce a preliminary version of'.
5. Morris, 17.
6. Osborne, B., 1995, 56.
7. Morris, 29.
8. Population figures for 1755, 1780, 1821 and 1825, Cleland 1825, p. 69. Figure for 1811, 1811 census quoted in Osborne, B., 26.
9. Hamilton, 1, 7; *Engineering: A History...*5; Riddell, 52–3.
10. Thus Cleland, 1825, p. 38. Regrettably he does not make clear whether this was the first steam engine in Glasgow and was installed in a cotton mill, or whether there were earlier engines for other

purposes and this was merely the first in a cotton mill. The former seems the more probable, at least so far as rotative engines are concerned.

11. Morris, 40.
12. Morris, 158; NLS ms 2675, notes of a conversation between John Buchanan and John Robertson, 1853, folio 22.
13. Osborne, J.C., 10.
14. Osborne, B., 1995, 51.
15. Correspondence between the author and B. Osborne; conversation between the author and Emily Malcolm, Curator Transport & Technology (Maritime and Engineering), Riverside Museum, Glasgow.
16. Osborne, B., 1995, 132.
17. For instance, in Chambers' *Edinburgh Journal*, 1839, quoted in Osborne, B., 1995, 67.
18. Blake, 75–6.
19. H. Philip Spratt, 'Bicentenary of Henry Bell' in *The Engineer*, 7 April 1967.
20. Morris, 29, 149; Osborne, B., 1995, 65–7.
21. Napier, 13, 16.
22. Osborne, B., 1995, 67–9.
23. *Statistical Account...*, 406; *New Statistical Account...*, Row, 82.
24. *New Statistical Account...*, Row, 79.
25. Osborne, B., 1995, 101, information derived from General Register of Sasines.
26. Durie, 66–9, 88–90; Stell, etc. (eds.) 374; Sherwood, 16; website http://en.wikipedia.org/wiki/Sea_bathing consulted on 20 Sept. 2011.
27. Ashworth, 46.
28. Osborne, B., 1995, 101.
29. Galt, 69, 71; Telford, 505 (appendix contributed by J. W. Gibb).
30. GMRC, Research Files relevant to Bell and the *Comet*, copy paper by Thomas Carswell, 'Memoir of Mr John Robertson, Engineer, Glasgow' 1864; Hughson, 9; Hughson, M., transcript of talk on Robertson, 2004, contained in bound volume *Notes and Correspondence collected by J. Craig Osborne during preparation of The Comet and her Creators*, Helensburgh Library; Osborne, B., 106; Osborne, J. C., 5, 24.
31. Noble (ed.), 176.
32. Osborne, B., 1995, 96–9.
33. Agnew, 10.
34. Osborne, B., 1995, 217–9; Ransom, 2004, 68–71.

Chapter Four:
The Genesis of the *Comet*

1. 47 G. III s.2, c.11.; Ransom, 169–171.
2. Kane, 40, quoting *Dumbarton Herald* 8 September 1859.
3. McLachlan, 36.
4. Improvement of the Clyde for navigation at the relevant period is covered in detail in Riddell 1–68, Hamilton 241–3 and Vernon-Harcourt 252–8.
5. Pennant, 134–7.
6. *New Statistical Account... Dunoon and Kilmun*, 608.
7. Morris, 28.
8. Woodcroft, 22, 32, 34.
9. Symington, 8; TNS, vol. 49 (1977–8), 143.
10. Morris, 30; Osborne, B., 1995, 137; Osborne, J. C., 5.
11. Bowman, A. I., 'The dockyard at Grangemouth', *Industrial Archaeology* vol. 16 no. 1, 1981, pp. 27–8.
12. Rankine, 8; Fox, 28.
13. Symington, 8.
14. *Caledonian Mercury*, 28 October 1816.
15. Spratt 1958, 85–6.
16. Letter from Bell to John McNeill, 1 March 1824, quoted in Woodcroft, 85. Another version of this letter, apparently embellished, is quoted in Morris, 74–5.
17. Mitchell, 131–2.
18. Dickinson, 256; Flexner, 349.
19. Osborne, B., 1995, 131.
20. E.g., Osborne, B., 1995, 134; Morris, 28–9.
21. NLS ms 2675, notes of a conversation between John Buchanan and John Robertson, 1853, folio 22.
22. Bell, 13.
23. Thomson, J., *Account of a Series of Experiments...*
24. Thomson, 4–11.
25. Hughson, 9–11; Osborne, J. C., 31; Spratt 1958, 87–8; H. Philip Spratt, 'Bicentenary of Henry Bell' in *The Engineer*, 7 April 1967.
26. GMRC, Research Files relevant to Bell and the *Comet*, copy paper by Thomas Carswell, 'Memoir of Mr John Robertson, Engineer, Glasgow' 1864; NLS ms 2675, notes of a conversation between John Buchanan and John Robertson, 1853, folio 22.

27. Napier, 13–14, 15–17, 77–8; GMRC, Research Files relevant to Bell and the *Comet*, copy letter from Napier D. to editor of *Glasgow Herald*, dated 18 December 1862.
28. Napier, 17.
29. *Henry Bell's "Comet"*, 12; *The Comet*, 40–2.
30. *Greenock Advertiser*, 9 June 1848, quoted in Osborne, J. C., 13; *Glasgow Herald*, 24 December 1860, quoted in Willamson, 12–13.
31. Bell, 14.
32. NLS ms 2675, notes of a conversation between John Buchanan and John Robertson, 1853, folio 23.
33. Napier, 17.
34. Reproduced in eg. Williamson, 14; Osborne, J. C., 29.
35. NLS ms 2675, notes of a conversation between John Buchanan and John Robertson, 1853, folio 24.
36. Somerville, 25.
37. Bell, 14–15.
38. NLS ms 2675, notes of a conversation between John Buchanan and John Robertson, 1853, folio 24.
39. Williamson, 282.
40. NLS ms 2675, notes of a conversation between John Buchanan and John Robertson, 1853, folio 23.
41. Website http://en.wikipedia.org/wiki/Great_Comet_of_1811 consulted 8 September 2011.
42. House of Commons Select Committee on Holyhead Roads, appendix 8, 224–5; NLS ms 2675, notes of a conversation between John Buchanan and John Robertson, 1853, folios 23–4; Osborne, B., 21, 27–8; Williamson, 282.

Chapter Five:
The *Comet* at Work – and her Competitors

1. NLS ms 2675, notes of a conversation between John Buchanan and John Robertson, 1853, folio 23.
2. Woodcroft, 81–2.
3. NLS ms 2675, notes of a conversation between John Buchanan and John Robertson, 1853, folios 23–4.
4. Macgeorge, 263.
5. E.g., in Kane, 139–45, Osborne J. C., 1–2, 28–33, 40–3; Watson, 42–3.

6. GMRC, Research Files relevant to Bell and the *Comet*, copy paper by Thomas Carswell, 'Memoir of Mr John Robertson, Engineer, Glasgow' 1864; NLS ms 2675, notes of a conversation between John Buchanan and John Robertson, 1853, folio 23; Telford, 506; Williamson, 7.

7. Osborne, J. C., 36.

8. *The Engineer*, 11 May 1877, quoted in Osborne, J. C., 52.

9. GMRC, Research Files relevant to Bell and the *Comet*, photocopy of registration certificate; Willliamson, 283.

10. Osborne, B., 1995, 153; Thomson, 19.

11. Woodcroft, 86.

12. *Edinburgh Evening Courant* 9 October 1813.

13. Osborne, J. C., 28; Thomson, 19–20.

14. Osborne, J. C., 42; Watson, 42, 43, 46.

15. Cleland, 1825, 59.

16. House of Commons Select Committee on Holyhead Roads, appendix 8, 224–5; Thomson, 16.

17. House of Commons Select Committee on Holyhead Roads, appendix 8, 224–5.

18. Dodd, xvii; NLS ms 2675, notes of a conversation between John Buchanan and John Robertson, 1853, folio 26.

19. E.g., Cleland, 1816, 396; House of Commons Select Committee on Holyhead Roads, appendix 8, 224; Williamson, 348.

20. E.g., Millar, 51; Napier, 107; Wood, 78.

21. Thomson, 17.

22. Thomson, 17.

23. Buchanan, 7, 34.

24. Bell, 20; *Edinburgh Evening Courant*, 9 October 1813; House of Commons Select Committee on Holyhead Roads, appendix 8, 224–5; Hughson, 12; Williamson, 23, 283.

25. *Edinburgh Evening Courant*, 9 October 1813; Haldane, 241.

26. Tann & Macleod, 11.

27. GMRC, Houldsworth Papers, T.1952.68.

28. Buchanan, 8; Cleland 1816, 392; Williamson, 23.

29. Napier, 18.

30. Napier, 106.

31. Buchanan, 165, plate XVI; Cleland 1825, 51–2; Millar, 53.

32. Smith, prelims page X.

33. Dickinson, 243, 318, plate opposite 317.

34. Buchanan, 167.

35. Millar, 53.
36. MPICE, vol V, 1846.
37. Cleland 1816, 396.
38. Hamilton, 210.
39. Cleland 1816, 396.
40. Cleland 1816, 396; Walker, 116; Williamson, 23–4.
41. GMRC, Houldsworth Papers, T.1952.68.
42. Millar, 53; Riddell, 75; Spratt, n.d., 15; Williamson, 23–5.
43. Millar, 53.
44. Millar, 53, 86; Spratt, n.d., 15.
45. Buchanan, xi, xii, 9, 24–27, 31, 34–5; Cleland 1816, 396–7; Dodd, xix.
46. Dyer, 285; Spratt 1958, 92–3; Walker, 116; Williamson, 331.
47. Buchanan, 24, 28, 165; Dodd, 244, 253, 255–6; Spratt 1958, 95.
48. Osborne, B., 1995, 165–6.
49. Dyer, 285; Spratt 1958, 94.
50. *A Biographical Dictionary of Civil Engineers...*, 183-4; *An Account of the Origin of Steam-Boats...*, 41; Dodd, 258; Spratt, 1958, 95–7.
51. Certain sources state that it was the *Glasgow*, rather than the *Argyle*, which became the *Thames* but this appears to be incorrect; likewise, some sources give the original name of *Argyle* as *Duke of Argyle*. Cleland, in *Annals of Glasgow*, published in 1816, is clear on pp 396–7 that *Argyle* was launched in 1814 and went to London in 1815; and Buchanan, in *A Practical Treatise on Propelling Vessels by Steam...*, also published in 1816, refers on page 173 to '...*Thames* (originally the *Argyle*...)'. Confusion has been made worse by the almost immediate re-use of the name *Argyle* for another steamboat, launched by John Wood & Co. in 1815. The earliest source seen by the present author to state that it was the *Glasgow* which became the *Thames* is the list of steamboats built 1812–1822 which appears in the appendix to the Fifth Report of the House of Commons Select Committee on Holyhead Roads, 1822. This was prepared by the well-known but London-based engineer Joshua Field, and omits all reference to the *Argyle* of 1814, although the 1815 vessel of that name is mentioned. It can be envisaged that one possible origin of the confusion might have been if *Argyle/Thames*, when working in the London area, became known colloquially as 'the Glasgow steamboat', i.e. the boat that originated in Glasgow.
52. Dodd, 255, 257, 259; *Glasgow Courier*, 13 May 1815, quoted in Osborne, B., 164.

53. Weld's account of the voyage is quoted in Dodd, 253–280.
54. Dodd, 245.

Chapter Six:
The Forth, the Tay and the Clyde

1. Harvey & Downs-Rose, 147; Osborne, B., 1995, 92.
2. Buchanan, 7.
3. Osborne, B., 98, 154.
4. Osborne, J. C., 40.
5. NAS, AC 7/95 Admiralty Court Decreets, Robert Paterson and Others against Henry Bell, 1818. The author is indebted to Stewart Noble for drawing attention to this source.
6. Buchanan, 61; Brodie 1976, 8.
7. Brodie 1976, 154, 156; Buchanan, 61–2; House of Commons Select Committee on Holyhead Roads, appendix 8, 198; NAS, AC 7/95 Admiralty Court Decreets, Robert Paterson and Others against Henry Bell, 1818.
8. NAS, AC 7/95 Admiralty Court Decreets, Robert Paterson and Others against Henry Bell, 1818.
9. Bell, H., in *Caledonian Mercury*, 28 October 1816; Cleland 1816, 397; Osborne, B., 1995, 160.
10. Osborne, 157–9.
11. Brodie 1976, 162; House of Commons Select Committee on Holyhead Roads, appendix 8, 199, 224–5; Lindsay, 39; Osborne, B., 1995, 160–1.
12. Buchanan, 62; Brodie 2003, 3, 4; Hughson, 12.
13. Buchanan, 62, 64, 172; Hughson 12–3; Scrowcroft, P. L., 'Passenger Boats on the River Don 1805–60' in JRHCS no. 197, March 2007, 532; Williamson, 20. Some sources state that *Caledonia* went into service between Hull and Selby, but Scowcroft, above, makes clear that the first route was Hull–Gainsborough.
14. Brodie 2003, 4; Gibb, 163, 246; Telford, 147, 234; Weir, 97, 101–3.
15. Weir, 68–9; 'Account of Mr Bald's Steam Passage Boat for the Alloa Ferry' in *Edinburgh Philosophical Journal*, 1822, reprinted in 'Pages from the Past' series by McCutcheon, Stirling, 1983.
16. Williamson, 29.
17. House of Commons Select Committee on Holyhead Roads, appendix 8, 224–5.

18. Napier, 19, 29, 51, 111.
19. NLS ms 2675, notes of a conversation between John Buchanan and John Robertson, 1853, folio 26.
20. Millar, 54.
21. Millar, 57–8, Williamson, 32.
22. Napier, 119; Williamson, 49, 321–30.
23. Cleland 1825, 61–2.
24. Morris, 59.
25. Hume & Moss, 16.
26. Cleland 1816, 398.
27. Williamson, 286–9.
28. Williamson, 28.
29. Cleland 1816, 394–5.
30. Dodd, xvii.
31. Buchanan, 11.
32. Williamson, 76.
33. Noble (ed.), 31.
34. Cleland 1816, 398–400.
35. Buchanan, 12–13; Williamson, 79.
36. Williamson, 53–5.
37. Riddell, 60, 99.
38. Riddell, 83–8, 100, 123.
39. de Selincourt (ed.), 375–9.
40. Durie, 69–71.
41. Galt, 73–43.
42. Ashworth, 88–9.
43. Napier, 20, 114–5.
44. *New Statistical Account of Scotland*, United parish of Dunoon and Kilmun, 606–8, 618.
45. Blake, 78, 81–2.
46. Gourvish, T. R. 'The Railways and Steamboat Competition in Early Victorian Britain' in *Transport History*, vol. 4., 1972, 2.
47. Gourvish, T. R. 'The Railways and Steamboat Competition in Early Victorian Britain' in *Transport History*, vol. 4., 1972, 8–12.

Chapter Seven:
The Way to Inverness – Bell's Last Great Scheme

1. Osborne, B. D. 2001, 13–17, 173–4.

2. Eleventh *Report of the Caledonian Canal Commissioners*, 1814, 34.

3. Lindsay, 126–8; Morris, 152–4.

4. GMRC, Research Files relevant to Bell and the *Comet*, photocopies of registration certificates; NLS ms 2675, notes of a conversation between John Buchanan and John Robertson, 1853, folios 24–5; Osborne, B. D. 1995, 171; Osborne, J.C., 42–3.

5. NLS ms 2675, notes of a conversation between John Buchanan and John Robertson, 1853, folios 24–5; Osborne, J. C., 43–4.

6. Osborne, B. D. 1995, 174.

7. *Glasgow Courier* 31 August 1819, reproduced in *Helensburgh Times* 4 September 1912, 9.

8. Osborne, B. D. 1995, 174.

9. *Glasgow Courier* 24 July 1819.

10. Osborne, B. D. 1995, 199.

11. Osborne, B. D. 1995, 172–83.

12. Osborne, B. D. 1995, 185, 210; Williamson, 32, 350.

13. Meek, D. E., 'Early Steamship Travel from the Other Side: An 1829 Gaelic Account of the *Maid of Morven*' in *Review of Scottish Culture*, no. 20, 57–79, John Donald, Edinburgh, 2008.

14. The whole subject is well covered by Meek, D. E. 'Steamships and Social Change in the Highlands and Hebrides, 1820–1955' in Veitch, K. (ed.), 227–273.

15. Osborne, B. D. 1995, 185–8.

16. Morris, 155.

17. Seventeenth *Report of the Caledonian Canal Commissioners*, 1820, 9.

18. Eighteenth *Report of the Caledonian Canal Commissioners*, 1821, 34.

19. Usually, contemporary references made to this vessel prior to 1820 refer to the *Stirling*, those made subsequently to the *Stirling Castle* (although, occasionally, to the *Stirling*). That there was one vessel not two is made clear by e.g. House of Commons Select Committee on Holyhead Roads, 118.

20. Osborne, B. D. 1995, 200; Mitchell, 131.

21. Morris, 155–6; Osborne, B. D. 1995, 191–2.

22. Account book, Glasgow Museums accession no. T.2006.51; Morris, 156; Osborne, B. D. 1995, 193–5.

23. Hume and Moss, 14; Osborne, B. D. 1995, 197; Williamson, 44–5, 350.

24. Duckworth & Langmuir, 3.

25. Mitchell, 68, 224; Nineteenth *Report of the Caledonian Canal Commissioners*, 1822, 18, 19.

26. Twentieth *Report of the Caledonian Canal Commissioners*, 1823, 3.
27. Twenty-First *Report of the Caledonian Canal Commissioners*, 1824, 37.
28. Lindsay, 157–9; Twentieth *Report of the Caledonian Canal Commissioners*, 1823, 11–19.
29. Twentieth *Report of the Caledonian Canal Commissioners*, 1823, 24–5.
30. Twentieth *Report of the Caledonian Canal Commissioners*, 1823, 25–6.
31. Lindsay, 160; Twenty-First *Report of the Caledonian Canal Commissioners*, 1824, 7.
32. Twenty-First *Report of the Caledonian Canal Commissioners*, 1824, 12.
33. Williamson, 288, 351.
34. Morris, 157; Osborne, B. D., 1995, 207–9; Williamson, 45–6.
35. Kane, 121.
36. Osborne, B. D., 1995, 204–7; Williamson, 46–9.
37. Kane, 36–40.
38. Osborne, B. D., 1995, 210–13; 2001, 220–3.
39. Duckworth & Langmuir, 3–4, 158–9.
40. du Toit, A., 'The Lochaber Archive Centre, Fort William' in *Scottish Archives: The Journal of the Scottish Record Association*, vol. 16, 2012, 102.
41. Mitchell, 224–5.
42. Duckworth & Langmuir, 36–7.
43. Pre-war steamer traffic and post-war cruising developments are well covered by Pedersen.

Chapter Eight:
The Mushroom Growth of Sheltered-Water Steamboats

1. Information from Rupa Kundu, British Science Association.
2. Smith, 16.
3. Hamilton, 10.
4. Flexner, 350–2; Smith, 16–17.
5. Spratt, *Marine Engineering*, 19, 25–7.
6. Beamish, 183, 347.
7. Napier, 23, 44, 60–1; Spratt, *Marine Engineering*, 18, 23.
8. Hills, 145–6.

9. Smith, 19, 25, 127, 129–33; Smith, E. C., 'The Centenary of Naval Engineering' in TNS, vol. II, 1921–2, 96–7; Spratt, *Marine Engineering*, 78; Williamson, 301.

10. Spratt, *Marine Engineering*, 103–7; Woodcroft, 105–8.

11. Dodd, XIX, XXI.

12. *Journal of the Society of Arts*, 30 March 1877, 446–7; 7 September 1877, 943–4; Malster, 59–61; Murray, M., 'Description of a Portable Steam Engine' in Nicholson, W., *A Journal of natural philosophy, chemistry and the arts* new series vol. XI, 1805, 95; Scott, 59.

13. Hadfield, 1972, 128.

14. *Journal of the Society of Arts*, 30 March 1877, 446.

15. *Journal of the Society of Arts*, 30 March 1877, 446; Malster, 62–4.

16. Dodd, XXIV; *Journal of the Society of Arts*, 30 March 1877, 446–7; Malster, 64.

17. Dodd, XXIV–XXV, 1–192.

18. Dodd, 193–9; House of Commons Select Committee on Steam Boats &c., 3–4.

19. Scott, 28.

20. Hughson, R. M., text of talk on John Robertson given March 2004, p. 5, contained in *Henry Bell and the Comet*, bound volume of notes and correspondence collected by J. Craig Osborne, held by Helensburgh Library.

21. Hadfield, 1970, 76; 1972, 129–30, 293.

22. GMRC, Houldsworth Papers, T.1952.68.

23. James, J. G., 'Ralph Dodd, The Very Ingenious Schemer' in TNS, vol. 47, 1977, 171–2; McMurray, 14–15.

24. Buchanan, 64; House of Commons Select Committee on Holyhead Roads, Fifth Report, 1822, 198–9; James, J. G., 'Ralph Dodd, The Very Ingenious Schemer' in TNS, vol. 47, 1977, 172; Tann & Macleod, 17–18.

25. Buchanan, 172, 174; Malster, 61.

26. Maudslay's career is well covered in Day & McNeil, 472–3; Gilbert 3–31; Rolt, 1962, 88–105.

27. Dodd, 228–9.

28. *The Funnel* (Journal of the Steam Boat Association of Great Britain), March 1982, page 26.

29. Dodd, 228–9.

30. Gilbert, 28.

31. House of Commons Select Committee on Holyhead Roads, Fifth Report, 1822, 198.

32. Dodd, 230–3.
33. Dodd, 234.
34. Dodd, XII; Sherwood, 16–19.
35. *An Account of the Origin of Steam-Boats...*, 37–9; Spratt, 1958, 93–4.
36. Sherwood, 22.
37. House of Commons Select Committee on Steam Boats &c, 29–30.
38. Dodd, XIII–XIV.
39. Dodd, 236–7.
40. *A Biographical Dictionary of Civil Engineers...*, 91; Beamish, 140–1; Buchanan, 63, 171, 173; Clements, 61; *The Funnel* (Journal of the Steam Boat Association of Great Britain), Dec. 1981, 196; Sherwood, 24.
41. Dodd, 238–40.
42. Dodd, 232, 235.
43. *An Account of the Origin of Steam-Boats...*, 43; House of Commons Select Committee on Holyhead Roads, Fifth Report, 1822, 199.
44. Spratt, 1958, 103–4; TNS vol. XXXII, 1959–60, 83–4; *The Funnel* (Journal of the Steam Boat Association of Great Britain), Dec. 1981, 196–7.
45. Sherwood, 13.
46. MPICE vol V, session 1846, presidential address by Sir John Rennie, given on 20 January 1846.
47. Sherwood, 80–1.
48. Body, 161–2, 193.
49. Hadfield, 1969 (South & South East England), 138, 144, 145; House of Commons Select Committee on Holyhead Roads, Fifth Report, 1822, 200.
50. TNS vol. 58, 1986–7, 130–1.
51. Buchanan, ix, 62; Dodd, 241; House of Commons Select Committee on Holyhead Roads, Fifth Report, 1822, 198; Woodcroft, 86.
52. Buchanan, 63; Hadfield, 1969 (West Midlands), 118.
53. Buchanan, 64; Delany, 119; Tann & Macleod, 15.
54. McNeill, 1965, 15, 40.
55. Delany, 119; Woodcroft, 86.
56. McNeill, 1967, 19, 23.
57. Buchanan, 64, Hadfield & Biddle, 94–5.
58. Jackman, 456.
59. Kavanagh, T., 'Early Steam Vessels on the River Dee, 1816-1827', Railway & Canal Historical Society, Waterway History Research Group, Occasional Paper 69, summer 2008.

60. *A Biographical Dictionary of Civil Engineers...*, 30; Buchanan, 175; Dickinson, 257–9; Spratt, 1958, 98–9; Watters, 63, 65, 66.
61. Spratt, 1958, 94–5.
62. House of Commons Select Committee on Holyhead Roads, Fifth Report, 1822, 226–7.
63. Spratt, 1958, 101–2; Spratt, n.d., 15–16.
64. Scott, 80; website www.tekniskamuseet.se consulted on 7 January 2012.
65. Dodd, 240; House of Commons Select Committee on Holyhead Roads, Fifth Report, 1822, 198; Tann & Macleod, 18–9; Watson, 6.
66. *A Biographical Dictionary of Civil Engineers...*, 555–6; Tann & Macleod, 19–20.
67. Tann & Macleod, 1, 20–2; Watson, 6–7.
68. J. Watt jun., quoted in Tann, 385.
69. Watson, 6–7.
70. *International Journal for the History of Engineering and Technology* v. 8, 201l, 12.

Chapter Nine:
The Seagoing Steamer Appears

1. Cleland, 1816, 400–1, Napier 17–8, 105–6.
2. Dodd, xix, Napier 18, 106.
3. Napier, 22–3, 32–3, 109.
4. Napier, 18, 52–4.
5. House of Commons Select Committee on Holyhead Roads, Fifth Report, 1822, 118.
6. Napier 52–3.
7. Morris, 7–8.
8. Pearson, 194.
9. Body, 29–30; website www.poheritage.com consulted 24 August 2011.
10. Meek, D. E., 'Steamships and Social Change in the Highlands and Hebrides' in Veitch (ed.), 232–3; Napier, 56–7; Watson, G., 'Early Steamship Voyages in the North' on website www.caithness.org consulted on 16 May 2007.
11. Napier, 52; House of Commons Select Committee on Holyhead Roads, Fifth Report, 1822, 118, 201.
12. Body, 62–3; House of Commons Select Committee on Holyhead

Roads, Fifth Report, 1822, 118, 201; website www.poheritage.com consulted on 24 August 2011.

13. Smith, 340.
14. Morris, 17.
15. Osborne, 1995, 116–20.
16. Dickinson, 182 et seq.
17. Dickinson & Titley, 78–9.
18. Osborne, 1995, 122.
19. Osborne, 1995, 113–5, 120, 122.
20. Scott, 28, 113.
21. See, e.g., Osborne, 115, Smith 82–4.
22. Dickinson, 182, 185.
23. Smith, 50–1; Tuckey, xiii, xxiii–xxvi.
24. Beamish 142–3; Smith, 51–2.
25. Boucher, 136.
26. *An Account of the Origin of Steamboats…*, 74; MPICE vol. V, session 1846, presidential address by Sir John Rennie, given on 20 January 1846; Smith, 52.
27. Smith, Eng. Capt. Edgar C., RN,"The Centenary of Naval Engineering' in TNS vol. II, 1921–2, 88, 107.
28. MPICE vol. V, session 1846, presidential address by Sir John Rennie, given on 20 January 1846; National Archives document ref. ADM 135/99; Smith, 52; Smith, Eng. Capt. Edgar C., RN, 'The Centenary of Naval Engineering' in TNS vol. II, 1921–2, 88, 106.
29. The voyages north and south are vividly described in *A Historical Account of His Majesty's Visit to Scotland*, 70–2, 76–86, 323–7; for *Queen Margaret* see Brodie, 1976, 157.
30. Smith, 19–22.
31. Smith, 91–2.
32. Smith, Eng. Capt. Edgar C., RN, 'The Centenary of Naval Engineering' in TNS vol. II, 1921–2, 106–8.
33. Philip, 349; Spratt, *c.* 1968, 10, 133.
34. Spratt, H. P., 'The Origin of Transatlantic Steam Navigation' in TNS v. 26, 1947–9, 134–5.
35. Spratt, H. P., 'The Origin of Transatlantic Steam Navigation' in TNS v. 26, 1947–9, 135–6.
36. Spratt, H. P., 'The Origin of Transatlantic Steam Navigation' in TNS v. 26, 1947–9, 136–7.
37. Smith, 22–6.
38. Smith, 85.

39. Rolt, 1957, 190–1.
40. Rolt, 1957, 197.
41. Smith, 42.
42. Smith, 45.
43. E.g., Fox, 70–83; Rolt, 1957, 191–200; Smith, 36–45.
44. Day & McNeil (eds.), 763; Lindsay, 39.
45. Allen, J. S., 'The History of the Horseley Company to 1865' in TNS v. 58, 1986–7, 121–2; Spratt, 1958, 13–6.
46. Delany, V. T. H. & D. R., 173–6; Petrie, J. F., 'Charles Wye Williams (1779–1866)' in TNS vol. xxxix, 1966–7, 35–7.
47. Ransom, 2004, 222–6.
48. Walker, 32; Williamson, 69, 352–3.
49. Walker, 32.
50. Hamilton, 220.
51. Rolt, 1957, 202–3; Smith, 64–71.
52. Smith, 73–4; Spratt, *Marine Engineering*, 113.
53. Hamilton, 219.
54. Brodie, 1976, 127.
55. Compound and Triple-expansion engines: with two, or three, cylinders, exhaust steam from one cylinder being re-used in the next.

Chapter Ten:
What Became of Bell – and What Became of the *Comet*

1. Morris, 41, 63; Osborne, B. D. (1995), 219–20.
2. Osborne, B. D., (1995), 220–3; Riddell, 170–1.
3. Napier, 82.
4. Napier, 31; NLS ms 2675, notes of a conversation between John Buchanan and John Robertson, 1853, folio 25; Osborne, B. D. (1995), 31–2; Osborne, J. C., 39, 41.
5. *New Statistical Account of Scotland*, Parish of Torphichen, 46.
6. Osborne, B. D. (1995), 106–9.
7. Morris, 63.
8. Cleland (1825) 59, Morris, 10.
9. Cleland (1825), 59, 61.
10. Morris, 7.
11. House of Commons Select Committee on Holyhead Roads, Fifth Report, 117–8.

12. Harvey & Downs Rose, 151–4; Miller (1862); Morris, 75–82; Osborne, B. D. (1995), 86–92; Woodcroft, 31–41, 57.

13. Morris, 8–14.

14. Morris, 9, 94–6, 119–20.

15. Morris, 13.

16. Morris, 61–2, 86–7, 90–4.

17. Morris, 92–3, 104–5.

18. Morris, 98, 104–5. This comment is sometimes attributed to the younger Brunel, Isambard Kingdom, but it is evident from Morris that it was spoken by the elder Brunel, Marc Isambard. In his lifetime the elder Brunel was known as 'Isambard', or 'Sir Isambard' after receiving his knighthood in 1841, three years before Morris's *Life of Henry Bell* was published. It is as 'I. Brunel', 'Mr Brunel' or 'Sir Isambard Brunel' that Morris refers to him. Today he is usually known as 'Marc', which name has been used by biographers writing about his son Isambard Kingdom Brunel, presumably to avoid confusion. Morris unfortunately muddies the waters by referring to Mr Brunel's son 'Charles' to whom he was introduced. Marc Isambard Brunel had only one son, Isambard Kingdom, who was about twenty years old at the date of Morris's visit. He eventually married in 1836 and in turn had two sons, Isambard and Henry Marc, and one daughter. The name 'Charles' appears to be a figment of Morris's imagination. [Sources: *A Biographical Dictionary of Civil Engineers in Britain and Ireland* Vol. 1: 1500–1830, pp 90–2; Rolt, L. T. C., *Isambard Kingdom Brunel* Longmans, Green & Co., 1957, pp 3–19, 99]

19. Lindsay, 113, 132; Morris, 129–33; Osborne, B. D. (1995) 230–4.

20. Lindsay, 132.

21. Lindsay, 137–9.

22. Morris, 136–40.

23. Noble (ed.), 207.

24. Osborne, B. D. (1995), 236, 247.

25. Morris, 61.

26. Osborne, B. D. (1995), 109–11.

27. Hughson, 13–14; NLS ms 2675, notes of a conversation between John Buchanan and John Robertson, 1853, folio 26; Williamson, 21.

28. Many sources [e.g. Hughson, 15; Morris, 41; Robinson, J. C. 'John Robertson, Builder of the engine for Henry Bell's *Comet*' in TNS vol. 49, 1977–8, 145; *The Story of Henry Bell's "Comet"*, 3] suggest or state that the original engine of the *Comet* was recovered

from the wreck in 1820. Despite this, it seems far more likely that it was taken out when the boat was lengthened. This is what Robertson said when interviewed in 1853 [NLS ms 2675, notes of a conversation between John Buchanan and John Robertson, 1853, folios 24–5], adding that 'thereafter' the *Comet* plied to Fort William. Some of what he said in this interview was clearly incorrect, for example that it was in the wreck of the *Comet* that Glengarry was killed, and indeed that the first *Comet* plied to Inverness: but he had a strong personal and continuing interest in the engine, and on that subject is likely to be correct. From a practical point of view, it would be surprising if the original engine, admittedly underpowered, were not replaced by a more powerful one at the time the boat was enlarged substantially for service in wilder waters than before. It also seems far more probable that an engine in a fit state to be sold for re-use would be one taken out of a vessel methodically during rebuilding, rather than one desperately recovered from a wreck in an inaccessible location. At remote Craignish, attempts at salvage could be made only by boat – probably by quite small boats, able to be beached on whatever strip of shingle lay not too far from the rocks onto which *Comet* had been driven. Maybe knowledge that attempts were made to recover the engine that was in the boat at the time of the wreck became, by a process akin to Chinese whispers, the 'fact' that the original engine had been recovered from it.

29. Morris, 41; NLS ms 2675, notes of a conversation between John Buchanan and John Robertson, 1853, folio 25; Riddell, 85, 275; Robinson, J. C. 'John Robertson, Builder of the engine for Henry Bell's *Comet*' in TNS vol. 49, 1977–8, 145; Williamson, 19; author's correspondence with British Science Association, 2011.

30. Hewish, 4, 7, 11–12, 31–2; Robinson, J. C. 'John Robertson, Builder of the engine for Henry Bell's *Comet*' in TNS vol. 49, 1977–8, 145–6.

31. Robinson, J. C. 'John Robertson, Builder of the engine for Henry Bell's *Comet*' in TNS vol. 49, 1977–8, 146.

32. Hewish, 32; Mitchell Library, Glasgow, accession no. 599617, 'MSS and printed material relating to William Symington … collected by Sir Charles Purcell Taylor'.

33. Robinson, J. C. 'John Robertson, Builder of the engine for Henry Bell's *Comet*' in TNS vol. 49, 1977–8, 146.

34. Hughson, 15–15; Osborne, J. C., 26; Robinson, J. C. 'John Robertson, Builder of the engine for Henry Bell's *Comet*' in TNS vol. 49, 1977–8, 146–8; Williamson, 19.

35. Spratt, H. P. 'Bicentenary of Henry Bell' in *The Engineer*, 7 April 1967, 515; correspondence between author and John Liffen, Curator of Communications, Science Museum, 2011.
36. Robinson, J. C. 'John Robertson, Builder of the engine for Henry Bell's *Comet*' in TNS vol. 49, 1977–8, 148.
37. Comet Centenary Celebration Committee.
38. Kelvingrove Museum and Art Gallery.
39. Ransom, 1989, 110–14; *The Comet*, 25–30. Much of the preceding four paragraphs appeared originally in the author's *Scottish Steam Today*, but since they are believed to be a concise and accurate account re-writing would serve no purpose. Those who wish to study the story of the replica *Comet* further may wish to note that there is (in 2011) a folder of correspondence and other relevant material in GMRC, Research Files relevant to Bell and the *Comet*.
40. Information from Inverclyde Council and Inverclyde Community Development Trust; websites http://cometrebuilt.blogspot.com/ and http://inverclydenow/ consulted November 2011.

Bibliography

A Biographical Dictionary of Civil Engineers in Britain and Ireland Vol. 1: 1500–1830, Thomas Telford Publishing, 2002.

A Historical Account of His Majesty's Visit to Scotland 2nd ed., Oliver & Boyd, Edinburgh, 1822.

Agnew, J., *The Story of the Vale of Leven* Famedram Publishers Ltd, Gartocharn, 1975.

An Account of the Origin of Steam-Boats in Spain, Great Britain and America; and of their Introduction and Employment upon the River Thames between London and Gravesend to the Present Time, Effingham Wilson, 1831. (Published anonymously: TNS vol. 47 pp 172 & 175 state the author to be Cruden, R. P.)

Ashworth, J. B., *The History of Helensburgh and Surrounding Area*, Portico Gallery, Helensburgh, 2001.

Baedeker, K., *Great Britain: A Handbook for Travellers* Karl Baedeker, Leipzig, 1910.

Beach, A. P., *Lake Champlain as Centuries Pass*, Lake Champlain Maritime Museum, Basin Harbor, 1994.

Beamish, R., *Memoir of the Life of Sir Marc Isambard Brunel* Longmans, Green, Longman & Roberts, 1862.

Bell, H., *Observations on the Utility of Applying Steam Engines to Vessels, &c.* J. Niven, Glasgow, 1813.

Bellico, R. P., *Sails and Steam in the Mountains: A Maritime and Military History of Lake George and Lake Champlain* Purple Mountain Press,

Fleischmanns, New York, 1992.

Birse, R. M., *Engineering at Edinburgh University* University of Edinburgh, Edinburgh, 1983.
Blake, G., *The Firth of Clyde* Collins, 1952.
Body, G., *British Paddle Steamers* David & Charles, Newton Abbot, 1971.
Boucher, C. T. G., *John Rennie 1761–1821: The Life and Work of a Great Engineer* Manchester University Press, Manchester, 1963.
Bowman, A. I., *Symington and the Charlotte Dundas* Falkirk Museums, Falkirk, 1981.
Brodie, I., *Steamers of the Forth* David & Charles, Newton Abbot, 1976.
Brodie, I., *Steamers of the Tay* Stenlake Publishing, Catrine, 2003.
Buchanan, R., *A Practical Treatise on Propelling Vessels by Steam &c.* Ackerman, 1816.

Cameron, A. D., *The Caledonian Canal* 3rd edition, Canongate Academic, Edinburgh, 1994.
Cleland, James, *Annals of Glasgow* vol. 2, Hedderwick, Glasgow, 1816.
Cleland, James, *Historical Account of the Steam Engine and its Application in Propelling Vessels* Khull, Blackie & Co., Glasgow, 1825.
Clements, P., *Marc Isambard Brunel* Longmans, 1970.
Comet Centenary Celebration Committee, *Celebration of launch of steamer "Comet", built for Henry Bell: official programme, 29th, 30th and 31st August, 1912* Aird & Coghill, Glasgow, 1912.

Day, L. and McNeil, I., (eds.) *Biographical Dictionary of the History of Technology* Routledge, 1996.
Delany, V. T. H. & D. R, *The Canals of the South of Ireland* David & Charles, Newton Abbot, 1966.
Delany, R., *The Grand Canal of Ireland* David & Charles, Newton Abbot, 1973.
de Selincourt, E., (ed.), *Journals of Dorothy Wordsworth* Vol. II, MacMillan & Co., 1941.
Dickinson, H. W., *Robert Fulton engineer and artist: His life and works* John Lane, the Bodley Head, 1913.
Dickinson, H. W., and Jenkins, R., *James Watt and the Steam Engine* Moorland Publishing Co. Ltd, Ashbourne, 1981 (first published 1927).
Dickinson, H.W., and Titley, A., *Richard Trevithick: The engineer and the man* Cambridge University Press, 1934.

Dodd, G., *An Historical and Explanatory Dissertation on Steam Engines and Steam Packets...* 1818.

Duckworth, C. L. D. & Langmuir, G. E., *West Highland Steamers* 3rd edition, T. Stephenson & Sons Ltd, Prescot, 1967.

Durie, A. J., *Scotland for the Holidays: Tourism in Scotland c1780–1939* Tuckwell Press Ltd, East Linton, 2003.

Dyer, J. C., 'Notes on the Introduction of Steam Navigation' in *Memoirs of the Literary and Philosophical Society of Manchester*, 3rd series, vol. II, 1865, 285.

Engineering: A History of its Development in the West of Scotland and a Guide to the Department in the Glasgow Art Gallery and Museum Glasgow Art Gallery and Museum, Glasgow, 1960.

Flexner, J. T., *Steamboats Come True: American Inventors in Action* second edition, Little, Brown & Company, Boston USA, 1978.

Fox, S., *The Ocean Railway* Harper Perennial, 2004.

Galt, J., *The Steam Boat* W. Blackwood, Edinburgh, 1822.

Gibb, Sir A., *The Story of Telford* Alexander Maclehose & Co., 1935.

Gilbert, K. R., *Henry Maudslay, Machine Builder* HM Stationery Office for Science Museum, 1971.

Hadfield, C., *British Canals* David & Charles, Newton Abbot, 4th ed. 1969.

Hadfield, C., *The Canals of South and South East England* David & Charles, Newton Abbot, 1969.

Hadfield, C., *The Canals of the East Midlands* David & Charles, Newton Abbot, 2nd ed. 1970.

Hadfield, C., *The Canals of the West Midlands* David & Charles, Newton Abbot, 2nd ed. 1969.

Hadfield, C., *The Canals of Yorkshire and North East England* David & Charles, Newton Abbot, 1972.

Hadfield, C., *Thomas Telford's Temptation* M & M Baldwin, Cleobury Mortimer, 1993.

Hadfield, C., & Biddle, G., *The Canals of North West England* vols. I & II (pages numbered consecutively through both vols.) David & Charles, Newton Abbot, 1970.

Haldane, A. R. B., *Three Centuries of Scottish Posts* Edinburgh University Press, Edinburgh, 1971.

Hamilton, H., *The Industrial Revolution in Scotland* Oxford University
    Press, Oxford, 1932.
Harvey, W. S. & Downs-Rose, G., *William Symington: Inventor and
    Engine Builder* Northgate Publishing Co. Ltd, 1980.
Henry Bell's "Comet" Lithgows Ltd, Port Glasgow, *c.* 1962.
Hewish, J., *The Indefatigable Mr Woodcroft: The legacy of invention* The
    British Library, *c.* 1979.
Hills, R. L., *Power from steam: A history of the stationary steam engine*
    Cambridge University Press, Cambridge, 1989.
House of Commons Select Committee on Holyhead Roads, Fifth Report,
    1822.
House of Commons Select Committee on Steam Boats, &c., Report, 1817.
Hughson, M., *John Robertson, Engineer* Barrhead & Neilston Historical
    Association, 1989.
Hume, J. R., & Moss, M. S., *A Bed of Nails: The history of P. MacCallum
    & Sons Ltd of Greenock, 1781–1981* Lang & Fulton, Greenock, *c.*
    1982.

Jackman, W. T., *The Development of Transportation in Modern England*
    Frank Cass & Co. Ltd, 3rd ed. 1966.

Kane, W, (compiler) *Follow the Comet's Tale* 2007 (bound volume of
    photocopies, etc. of material relating to the first and second *Comets*,
    held by Helensburgh Library).
Kelvingrove Museum and Art Gallery *Descriptive Catalogue, centenary
    exhibition, British steam navigation, Kelvingrove Museum...*
    Corporation of Glasgow, Glasgow, 1912.

Lindsay, J., *The Canals of Scotland* David & Charles, Newton Abbot,
    1968.

Macgeorge, A., *Old Glasgow: the Place and the People* Blackie & Son,
    Glasgow, 1880.
McLachlan, G., *The Story of Helensburgh* Macneur and Bryden,
    Helensburgh, n.d.
McMurray, H. C., *Old Order, New Thing* HM Stationery Office for
    National Maritime Museum, 1972.
McNeill, D. B., *Coastal Passenger Steamers and Inland Navigations in the
    North of Ireland* Belfast Transport Museum, 2nd impression, 1967.
McNeill, D. B., *Coastal Passenger Steamers and Inland Navigations in the*

South of Ireland Belfast Transport Museum, 1965.

Malet, H., *Bridgewater: The Canal Duke, 1736–1803* Manchester University Press, Manchester, 1977.

Malster, R., *Wherries and Waterways* Terence Dalton Ltd, Lavenham, 1971.

Millar, W. J. 'On Early Clyde Built Steamers' in *Transactions of the Institution of Engineers and Shipbuilders in Scotland* vol. xxiv, 1880–1.

Miller, W. H., *A Letter to Bennet Woodcroft, Esq. F.R.S. vindicating the right of Patrick Miller Esq. of Dalswinton to be regarded as the first inventor of practical steam navigation* Whittingham and Wilkins, 1862.

Minutes of Proceedings of the Institution of Civil Engineers (MPICE).

Mitchell, J., *Reminiscenses of my Life in the Highlands* vol. I, David & Charles (Publishers) Ltd, Newton Abbot, 1971 (re-issue of original edition published 1883).

Morris, E., *The Life of Henry Bell, The Practical Introducer of the Steam-Boat into Great Britain and Ireland...* Blackie, Glasgow, 1844; Kessinger Publishing facsimile available, print-on-demand, from Amazon, 2011.

Napier, D., with additional material by Bell, D., *David Napier Engineer 1790–1869: An Autobiographical Sketch with Notes* James Maclehose and Sons, Glasgow, 1912. (n.b. The autobiographical 'Memoir by David Napier', which appears to have been written in the late 1840s, occupies pp 15–28. The remainder of the text, i.e. pp 1–14 and 29–126, is mostly the work of David Bell, but includes material quoted from other earlier sources.)

New Statistical Account of Scotland, Parish of Row, 1839.

New Statistical Account of Scotland, Parish of Torphichen, *c.* 1840.

New Statistical Account of Scotland, United parish of Dunoon and Kilmun, 1843.

Noble, S., (ed.) *200 Years of Helensburgh 1802–2002* Helensburgh Heritage Trust/Argyll Publishing, Glendaruel, 2002.

Osborne, B. D., *The Ingenious Mr Bell* Argyll Publishing, Glendaruel, 1995.

Osborne, B. D., *The Last of the Chiefs* Argyll Publishing, Glendaruel, 2001.

Osborne, J. C., *The Comet and her Creators* published by the compiler, 2007.

Paterson, L., *From Sea to Sea* Neil Wilson Publishing Ltd, Glasgow, 2006.

Pearson, H., *Sir Walter Scott, His Life and Personality* House of Stratus, 2001.

Pedersen, R. N., *Loch Ness with Jacobite* Inverness, 2007.

Pennant, T., *A Tour in Scotland and Voyage to the Hebrides 1772 1776* edition re-issued by Birlinn Ltd, Edinburgh, 1998.

Philip, C. O., *Robert Fulton: A Biography* Franklin Watts, New York, 1985.

Prager, F. D., (ed.) *The Autobiography of John Fitch* American Philosophical Society, Philadelphia, 1976.

Rankine, J. and W. H. *A Biography of William Symington, Civil Engineer* A. Johnstone, Falkirk 1862.

Ransom, P. J. G., *Loch Lomond and The Trossachs in History and Legend* John Donald, Edinburgh, 2004.

Ransom, P. J. G., *The Archaeology of the Transport Revolution 1750–1850* World's Work Ltd, Tadworth, 1984.

Ransom, P. J. G., *Scottish Steam Today* Richard Drew Publishing, Glasgow, 1989.

Reports of the Commissioners for Making and Maintaining the Caledonian Canal (Parliamentary Papers) – cited as '*Reports of the Caledonian Canal Commissioners*'

Riddell, J. F., *Clyde Navigation: A History of the Development and Deepening of the River Clyde* John Donald Publishers Ltd, Edinburgh, 1979.

Rolt, L. T. C., *Isambard Kingdom Brunel* Longmans, Green and Co., 1957.

Rolt, L. T. C., *Great Engineers* G. Bell and Sons, Ltd, 1962.

Scott, E. K., (ed.) *Matthew Murray: Pioneer Engineer* TEE Publishing, Warwickshire, 1999 (first published 1928).

Shaw, J., Stell, G., and Storrier, S., (eds.) *Scottish Life and Society* vol. 3 *Scotland's Buildings* Tuckwell Press, East Linton, 2003.

Sherwood, T., *The Steamboat Revolution: London's first Steamships* Tempus Publishing Ltd, Stroud, 2007.

Smith, Capt. E. C., *A Short History of Naval and Marine Engineering* Babcock and Wilcox, Ltd, Cambridge, 1937.

Somerville, C., *Colour on the Clyde* Bute Newspapers Ltd, Rothesay, 3rd ed. 1970.

Spratt, H. P., *The Birth of the Steamboat* Charles Griffin & Co. Ltd, 1958.

Spratt, H. P., *Science Museum: Handbook of the Collections illustrating Marine Engineering* Her Majesty's Stationery Office, n.d. (reprint of 1953 edition with amendments).

Spratt, H. P., *Science Museum: Handbook of the Collections illustrating Merchant Steamers and Motor-Ships* part II, Her Majesty's Stationery Office, *c.* 1968 (reprint of 1948 ed. with addenda).

Stanhope, G. & Gooch, G. P., *The Life of Charles, Third Earl of Stanhope* Longmans, Green & Co., 1914.

Statistical Account of Scotland, parish of Row, 1791–9.

Symington, W., *A Brief History of Steam Navigation* Falkirk, 1829 (reissued 1863).

Tann, J., (ed.) *The Selected Papers of Boulton & Watt* vol. 1, *The Engine Partnerships*, Diploma Press, 1981.

Tann, J., & Macleod, C., *Empiricism Afloat – Testing Steamboat Efficacy: Boulton Watt & Co. 1804–1830* paper presented at XIV International Economic History Conference, Helsinki 2006, Session 38.

Telford, T., ed. Rickman, J., *Life of Thomas Telford* J. & L. G. Hansard, 1838.

The Comet Port Glasgow Town Council, Port Glasgow, 1962.

The first practical steamboat: William Symington and the Charlotte Dundas, Scottish Industrial Heritage Society, Grangemouth, 2003.

The Official Descriptive and Illustrated Catalogue of the Great Exhibition of the Works of Industry of all Nations, 1851 Spicer Brothers, 1851.

The Story of Henry Bell's "Comet" Comet Trust, Port Glasgow, 1962.

Thomson, J., *Account of a Series of Experiments made for the Purpose of Ascertaining the Best Mode of Constructing Vessels with Machinery, to be wrought on Navigable Rivers by the Power of Steam* Mennons Co., Glasgow, 1813.

Transactions of the Newcomen Society (TNS)

Tuckey, Capt. J. K., RN, *Narrative of an Expedition to Explore the River Zaire usually called the Congo in South Africa in 1816* John Murray, 1818.

Veitch, K., (ed.) *Scottish Life and Society* vol. 8 *Transport and Communications* John Donald, Edinburgh, 2009.

Vernon-Harcourt, L. F., *Rivers and Canals* vol. I, Oxford University Press, 2nd edition 1896.

Walker, F. M., *Song of the Clyde: A history of Clyde shipbuilding* Patrick Stephens Ltd, Cambridge, 1984.

Watson, D., *From* Comet *to* Caledonia, Brown, Son & Ferguson, Glasgow, 1999.

Watters, B., *Where Iron runs like Water!: A New History of Carron Iron Works 1759–1982* John Donald Publishers Ltd, Edinburgh, 1998.

Williamson, J. W., *Clyde Passenger Steamers 1812–1901*, 1904, re-issued in facsimile, Spa Books Ltd, Stevenage, 1987.

Weir, M., *Ferries in Scotland* John Donald, Edinburgh, 1988.

Wood, J. L., 'Scottish Marine Engineering: the First Fifty Years' in *Transactions of the Newcomen Society*, vol. 64, 1992–3.

Woodcroft, B., *A Sketch of the Origin and Progress of Steam Navigation* Taylor, Walton, and Maberley, 1848.

Index